The Marketing Game!
Second Edition

Charlotte Mason
William D. Perreault, Jr.
Both of
University of North Carolina at Chapel Hill

IRWIN

Chicago • Bogota • Boston • Buenos Aires • Caracas
London • Madrid • Mexico City • Sydney • Toronto

ISBN 0-256-17863-1

2 3 4 5 6 7 8 9 0 ML 1 0 9 8 7 6 5

About the Authors

CHARLOTTE H. MASON is an Associate Professor of Marketing at the Kenan-Flagler Business School, University of North Carolina at Chapel Hill. She received her Ph.D. from Stanford University in 1985. Prior to her academic career, Dr. Mason worked at Procter and Gamble—where her major responsibilities focused on designing and programming simulations used in strategic planning. Following that experience, she worked as a consultant for Booz Allen—where she was also involved in developing simulations for Booz Allen's clients. Dr. Mason's research specialization in marketing is the development of marketing models. In fact, *The Marketing Game!* simulation builds on her research on modeling the demand for new products. Her recent publications include articles in *Marketing Science*, *Journal of Marketing Research*, and *Marketing Letters*. She is also a frequent contributor to national conferences, and serves on the editorial review boards of several major journals, including the *Journal of Marketing Research* and *Journal of Marketing*.

WILLIAM D. PERREAULT, JR. is Kenan Professor of Business Administration at the Kenan-Flagler Business School, University of North Carolina at Chapel Hill. He is coauthor, with E. J. McCarthy, of two other widely used marketing texts—*Basic Marketing* and *Essentials of Marketing*. Dr. Perreault has been developing and working with marketing simulations for 20 years—both in the classroom and in industry. He has published many articles on computer applications in marketing education and marketing management. He has also served as the editor of the *Journal of Marketing Research* and on the editorial review board for a number of other journals. Dr. Perreault has worked as a consultant to major firms that market software and computers—and he is the developer of a software system that is widely used in marketing research organizations.

Preface

We are indeed excited about this new second edition of *The Marketing Game!* And we hope you will be too. It includes many new innovations and improvements that build on the success of our original simulation.

Eight years ago, we started work on the first edition of *The Marketing Game!* Our aspiration was not just to improve on other competitive marketing simulations that had been available in the past, but rather to pioneer a new generation of simulations. We wanted the game to be flexible, so it would effectively serve a wide variety of marketing teaching and learning needs, from the most basic to the most sophisticated. We wanted it to be the best simulation in the world, and at the same time the easiest to use—so it would be attractive to people who had never previously considered teaching with a simulation. We wanted to design it to be rich in student interest and realism, and yet to create a strategy planning environment where random events would not mask the relationship between good decisions and results achieved. No one learns anything in situations like that, but they were all too typical of most simulations. We also wanted participants both to have fun and be challenged analyzing the results of the simulation and planning new strategies, while at the same time making it fast and easy for instructors to *diagnose* how participants were progressing. In sum, our wish list in preparing the first edition of the game appeared to represent a tall order!

It is indeed gratifying that the game has proved so successful—and that students and instructors alike have been enthusiastic about what we achieved toward our original objectives. At the same time, creative colleagues at hundreds of colleges, universities, and companies who had worked with the first edition of the game for a number of years came up with a host of great ideas on ways to make it even better. We are grateful to the many students and faculty who have shared suggestions, criticisms and ideas about ways to improve or update this student manual, the student and instructor software, and the other instructor materials that accompany the simulation. Our most ardent supporters and loyal users have often been our best critics!

In the spirit of the first edition, this new second edition of *The Marketing Game!* is designed to provide the basis for a high-involvement learning experience. It's fun. But it is also challenging. The focus is on effective marketing strategy planning in a competitive environment. It gives you the opportunity to analyze markets and target market needs. You make decisions in a number of strategy decision areas—to develop a marketing plan that satisfies your target market and earns a profit for your firm. If you wish, you can use the PLAN software that comes with this manual to more easily and quickly evaluate the budget and financial implications of your strategy.

It has been a priority to make the simulation—and the market environment—realistic. Firms compete by developing and marketing one or more software products—and supporting customers with service after-the-sale. Marketing managers select and focus on target markets from among a variety of business and consumer segments—and reach their targets with different channels. Promotion—including personal selling, advertising and sales promotion—must consider middlemen and final customers. Prices must be set to offer customers the value they seek and yield profits for the firm. The simulation starts in the growth stage of the product life cycle—and continues into market maturity. R&D decisions make it possible to modify the product(s) over time to better meet customer needs and competitive challenges. The game can continue for as many decision periods as the instructor desires. The instructor also has a variety of optional ways to "set up" or adjust the market environment to meet specific teaching and learning objectives.

Both the text and computer simulation have been carefully written to build on the marketing strategy planning framework and the 4Ps organization pioneered by E. Jerome McCarthy. This organization is used in *Basic Marketing*—the most widely used text in marketing. But, importantly, it has been adopted and used in almost every other marketing text. Moreover, because this framework really works, it has become the cornerstone of marketing strategy planning in most firms. By building on this standard we ensure that the simulation will work well in a variety of learning and teaching situations—and with students who have different levels of knowledge and experience—whether the students are just learning about marketing or are seasoned executives.

In fact, this flexibility is possible because the game is not based on just one simulation, but several simulations within one integrated framework. It has been specially designed so that the instructor can select the number of decision areas—and increase the number of decision areas (and thus the difficulty level) over time. This innovation, introduced with the first edition of the game, is one reason the game has quickly became one of the most widely used marketing simulations in the world. It is why the game works well whether it is used with senior executives in management development programs, with undergraduate and graduate students in the first marketing course, or with students in electives such as marketing strategy and product management.

One of the key advantages of using a simulation rather than some other realistic learning approach—such as case discussions or industry studies—is that it provides immediate feedback. Even in the real world feedback is often slow—and mistakes can certainly be very costly. In contrast, with a well-designed simulation, strategies can be formulated and then tested and refined over time. The experience and learning that result are cumulative.

We have designed *The Marketing Game!* to ensure that these pedagogical benefits are realized. It is set in a dynamic market environment. Thus, a poor decision early in the competition does not frustrate the learning process or leave a student/manager with poor results from then on. New decision periods bring opportunity for new successes. And firms with early successes can't coast on their laurels, but must constantly "earn" their customers' business. Thus, there is ample opportunity to learn from both successes and mistakes.

In addition, this is not a narrowly defined market in which success by one firm dooms others to failure. There are a number of different types of opportunities to pursue. Each firm can develop its own effective and profitable marketing strategy. As in the real world, the marketing manager in the game decides whether to compete head-on with other firms or pursue a niche with less competition. Either way, however, good decisions produce good results. As simple as that sounds, it is perhaps the single greatest strength of this simulation—and where so many others fall short.

Moreover, this is not a "zero sum" game—one in which one competitor must lose for another one to win. While many other simulations rely on the assumptions of zero sum competition, we believe that approach fails to consider the pedagogical reasons for using a simulation in the first place. It simply doesn't make sense to assume that if one student participant does a good job that another must be doing a bad job. In *The Marketing Game!*, good work and smart decisions are reinforced with good outcomes—and that reinforces the learning process for everyone involved.

A marketing budget for each firm in each period highlights the trade-offs among marketing expenditures that marketing managers must make when developing a marketing strategy. A "smart" marketing strategy must be based on a marketing mix that is consistent with target market needs—but that doesn't mean that it must be a high-cost strategy.

The text includes budget planning and marketing strategy forms that help develop skills in analyzing alternative marketing plans. These can be used by themselves or in combination with the accompanying PLAN software, which is discussed in Appendix A at the end of this text.

There is a very complete *Instructor's Manual to Accompany The Marketing Game!* The manual gives many suggestions to help make the simulation a successful teaching/learning experience for instructors and students alike.

We have made hundreds of revisions and improvements in the simulation software, the instructor materials, and in this book. We won't catalog all of the changes here. After all, a long "what's new" list probably isn't relevant for most students who are participating in the game for the first time. But instructors who have used the game in the past will find a detailed list of the changes at the beginning of the revised instructor's manual.

Our students—and hundreds of our colleagues from around the world who teach with the game—report that *The Marketing Game!* is an exciting and integrating learning experience. Our sincere hope is that you will have the same reaction.

Acknowledgments

Many people have made important contributions to *The Marketing Game!*

We owe the greatest debt to our students—in undergraduate, graduate, and executive program courses—who used "beta test" versions of this edition of *The Marketing Game!* Their enthusiasm about the experience—and what they were learning—was an important motivator for us. In addition, the thousands of marketing plans that they have submitted over the past few years helped us to refine and improve the simulation. And their questions and suggestions gave us ideas on ways to improve the text.

We especially appreciate the many faculty—and it is perhaps a hundred or more at this point—who have taken the time and initiative to write or call with detailed suggestions concerning *The Marketing Game!* Hopefully, these valued colleagues will see that we have taken their expert inputs seriously. The vast majority of the changes in this new edition were stimulated by the suggestions they provided.

We are grateful to our faculty colleagues and current and past doctoral candidates at the Kenan-Flagler Business School. They have been eager supporters of the game, and in our own "backyard" have demonstrated a wide variety of creative new ways to use the game. It's often said that "imitation is the sincerest form of flattery." So our colleagues should be flattered that many of their creative ideas are now incorporated in the game and supporting materials.

During the past 7 years we have been invited to give many presentations and participate in a variety of workshops, consortia, conferences, and institutes concerning the use of simulations in marketing education. These events have spanned a number of countries, and organizations ranging from the Marketing Education Group in the U.K., A.M.A. and other professional societies in the U.S., and associations such as the American Assembly of Collegiate School of Business. We appreciate the the opportunity to share our ideas at these gatherings. They have given us a chance to fine-tune our thinking and benefit from the criticisms and ideas of many other thoughtful participants.

We would like to thank our families for all of their support. Jeff Eischen provided support and encouragement throughout the project. We appreciate his suggestions for ways to resolve computer programming problems as well as his ideas on the text. Pam Perreault was also very helpful; she read a number of drafts of the text, and offered many valuable suggestions after each reading.

Finally, we would like to thank our publisher. The people at Richard D. Irwin, Inc. provided much valuable support—from the very beginning of the project through the final printing process.

To all of these people—and to others who have encouraged us along the way—we are deeply grateful. Responsibility for any errors or omissions is certainly ours, but *The Marketing Game!* would not have been possible without the support of many others.

Table of Contents

1
Introduction to THE MARKETING GAME!

PLANNING MARKETING STRATEGY

Planning and implementing a marketing strategy is exciting—and challenging. To develop effective strategies, a marketing manager must analyze available market opportunities, understand and select target markets, and develop a marketing mix that will give the firm an advantage over competitors. Many decisions are involved, and each decision relates to all of the others. The fact that there is never a single right answer adds to the challenge—and to the opportunities.

Competition Makes a Difference

Competition is part of what makes marketing exciting. Financial managers for different firms can use the same formula for figuring the return on an investment or the discounted present value of the investment. Accountants for competing firms can use the same commonly accepted practices in setting up their accounting records. Competing companies may use the same approaches for motivating employees. But, if marketing managers for competing firms use the same strategy, the competition just becomes more intense. What will work—and work well—for an individual firm depends on the whole market—what needs customers have as well as how other competing firms are trying to meet those needs.

Traditional approaches to learning about marketing strategy planning—reading about it in texts and articles, analyzing case situations, and working problems and exercises—can be very effective. These approaches provide the framework and tools that you need to make good decisions. But it is difficult for these approaches to give you a complete opportunity to put it all together—to put you in the driver's seat. That kind of learning experience comes from making decisions—and then seeing the results of your decisions.

Putting It All Together

That's where The Marketing Game! comes in—with a solution. It gives you an opportunity to *learn by doing*. You are the marketing manager for your firm. You analyze customers and their needs. You plan strategies—selecting target markets and blending product, place, promotion and price (the 4 Ps) to develop a competitive advantage in the market. Of course, identifying a competitive advantage also requires an understanding of competitors and their strengths and weaknesses.

In other words, you experience the excitement of being deeply involved in turning a market opportunity into results for your firm. And feedback about your results, competitors and customers gives you the opportunity to constantly improve your strategy. In sum, the game provides you with hands-on experiences that bring marketing concepts and ideas alive. It's fun. It's also challenging.

You might be wondering how all of these good things can be accomplished. It's a good question. And there's a straightforward answer. You make it happen. You bring it to life.

The pages that follow set the stage—and provide the background you need to bring the marketing management job to life. When you—and the managers for other firms—have made decisions, a computer program analyzes all of the decisions and provides you with detailed feedback about what would have happened in a real marketplace. You don't need to know about the details of the computer program. In fact, after these first few pages you won't hear much about the role of the computer in the Marketing Game! Rather, you will focus on understanding the market—and on making important decisions for your firm.

Reading the Text

You will quickly find that this book is *not* like other texts. In many ways, the book is like an extended case study. The chapters are written as if they were a set of internal company reports and memos. These reports are not directed to you in your role as a student—they are directed to you in your role as marketing manager for the firm. The reports provide information about the market, the company, and your responsibilities—information you need to do your marketing management job.

Enough on that. Now, let's get on with the responsibilities of your new job.

WHAT'S AHEAD

You Are the New Marketing Manager

From now on, you can think of yourself as a new manager who has just joined the firm. At present, the firm develops and markets computer programs (software) for a special type of microcomputer. The previous marketing manager helped get the firm started, but he has now retired and the company wants you to take charge of its marketing effort—and help guide it in the decade ahead.

The President of the Firm Is Your Boss

Your instructor is the president of your firm. Like other top managers, you are responsible to the president of your firm. You will provide the president with your recommendations and decisions—and the president will help coordinate things with other departments as needed. For example, the president will make certain that the accounting department provides you with the financial summaries you need—and that you have a reasonable budget based on your contributions to the firm. The president will work with the production people to make certain that they produce the product you want for your target market and that it is available on schedule.

The president may even expand your responsibilities—giving you authority to make decisions that are now based on company policy. For example, the president may give you the authority to introduce a totally new product, take over planning of sales promotion that is currently handled by an outside firm specializing in this area, or alter the way in which sales reps are paid.

To help you get off to a fast start in your new job, the president has given you this book—so you have the specific information you need to make good decisions. Before moving on to the specifics, however, it might be helpful for you to get an overview of what you will find in the upcoming chapters.

Chapter 2—The Market Opportunity

The president hired you to help bring a marketing orientation to the firm. Because you do not have previous experience with this firm—or its product, customers and competitors—the president has hired an consulting firm to prepare a report for your review. The president told the consultants that the report should provide an objective outside view of the market and company—to help you get up to speed faster.

Chapter 2 is the report prepared by the consulting firm. It describes the broad product market in which the firm competes. It also discusses how firms in the market have operated in the past—and why. Directly and indirectly it also outlines some of the challenges and opportunities that need to be considered in developing effective marketing mixes and selecting a target market. [Note: At the time of this writing, generally available microcomputer software and hardware has not evolved to the extent that is portrayed in Chapter 2; yet, the product market described is consistent with a direction that computing is taking. Thus, the product market situation is realistic and interesting—but still requires that you base your decisions on the information in this book and in the reports you receive, not on the way you think some computer software company may have handled the challenge in the past.]

Chapter 3—Marketing Department Responsibilities

You were hired because the previous marketing manager retired. When he announced his intention to retire, the president asked him to prepare a transition report—so that the new person who took over as marketing manager would know more about the marketing department's areas of responsibility.

Chapter 3 is the memo prepared by the previous marketing manager. It reviews company policies that affect the marketing department and explains some of the details of what needs to be considered in developing a marketing plan for the firm. It also discusses different marketing research reports and studies that are available to help you better understand your customers and competitors, and how you are doing in the market.

Chapter 4—Submitting the Annual Marketing Plan

As marketing manager, you need to develop marketing strategy and marketing plans for the future. Of course, these may need to be revised and updated each year to take into consideration feedback about how well the strategy is working, what competitors are doing, and other changes in the market.

At the beginning of each year, you will submit your marketing plan. The president has asked that the key decisions in your plan be summarized on a Marketing Plan Decision Form. The form will make it easy for the president to review your plan because it summarizes the key decisions you'll make in each of your areas of responsibility.

A staff assistant in the president's office has prepared a set of notes that explain the Marketing Plan Decision Form. The assistant has also prepared samples of the various company reports and marketing research reports that are available to you.

Chapter 4 is the report prepared by the president's assistant. It includes important information about the firm's current financial situation and a summary of the results produced by the previous year's marketing plan. It is the starting point on which you will build your decisions.

Chapter 5—Submitting an Expanded Marketing Plan

The president has been considering several changes in company policy—and these changes could have a direct effect on the marketing department and your responsibilities as marketing manager.

The president asked one of his assistants to prepare a brief memo that outlines the changes he has in mind. At the early point when the draft memo was prepared, the president had not made a final decision about the changes being considered.

However, the president wanted to have the ideas in writing so that everyone could move quickly once the final decision was made.

Chapter 5 is the memo prepared by the president's assistant. The president may instruct you to read Chapter 4 and follow the guidelines established there—or instead to rely on the expanded guidelines presented in Chapter 5. In either event, the materials are ready and waiting for the president's decision.

Chapter 6—Supporting the Marketing Plan

The Marketing Plan Decision Form that you will submit to the president each year provides a concise summary of the key decisions in your marketing plan. The president may also ask for other supporting information about the strategy on which the plan is based and what results you expect the plan to achieve.

A member of the president's staff has prepared several forms that will help you submit such supporting information. Chapter 6 is the material that the president's assistant has put together for you. It includes copies of a Marketing Strategy Summary Form and a Marketing Budget Planning Form—along with brief ideas on how each might be used.

The president may or may not ask you to complete these forms and submit a copy with your marketing plan. Either way, summarizing your ideas on these forms can help you to develop a better marketing plan—and make more effective use of your budget. And the completed forms will help you keep an organized record of your decisions over time.

Chapter 7—A New Market Opportunity

Chapter 7 is a second report prepared by the same outside consulting firm that prepared Chapter 2. At the end of that first report, the consultants mentioned that there might be a good opportunity for the firm to develop a completely new product. After reading the first report, the president asked the consultants to elaborate on their ideas in a report that detailed the pros and cons of the firm expanding its product line to include a new offering. The consultants have uncovered some interesting information. But at the same time, they conclude that the final decision about introducing a new product rests with the president—since any move in that direction will require additional resources and will lead the firm in new directions. The president has not yet decided if the firm should introduce the new product. The president may ask for your recommendations in that area—or even give you the authority to handle the decision yourself.

Appendix A—Decision Support System

Finally, Appendix A was prepared by the information systems department. At the request of the previous marketing manager, the data processing specialists developed a microcomputer program that would make it faster to submit an electronic version of the marketing plan decision form—and easier to do some of the financial calculations and projections that are useful in marketing planning. The appendix provides instructions on using the computer program.

You are starting a new job, and you have a number of new areas of responsibility. As a result, the president may recommend that you get started without relying on the computer program. It's easy to use, but the same analyses can be done in other ways. For example, you can use the Marketing Budget Planning Form in Chapter 6 to do several of the analyses that are handled by the computer program.

IN CONCLUSION

The reports that are provided in the following chapters will give you a lot of useful information about your new job. The challenge is to analyze the opportunities and—within the constraints of your firm's resources—to develop a profitable marketing mix. You will find many useful hints as you study the reports, and you will get other insights as you get feedback on the results of your plan decisions. So, we won't give you much other advice here. But, one general piece of advice is important. Specifically, just as is the case in the business world, you should know that there is not some "trick" or single "correct answer" in planning strategies for the game. There are a number of ways to succeed. And the best marketing plan depends on what target market you go after, and on what competitors are doing. Finally, as in the real world, success by one firm doesn't doom a competing firm to failure. To the contrary, there are many opportunities for success in *The Marketing Game!*

We hope you will enjoy your new responsibilities. You face some interesting opportunities and challenges. We are confident that you will do the job well.

2
THE MARKET OPPORTUNITY

Note: The president of your firm asked Market-Views, Inc.— a consulting firm— to prepare a report that would give you a concise but objective view of your company and the market in which it competes. This chapter is Market-Views' report.

INTRODUCTION

Your firm currently develops and markets a special software product for microcomputers. But the purpose of this report is not just to focus on what the company produces—or how it currently operates. Rather, the objective is to provide you with a broader view of the market in which your firm competes. Understanding the market, your competitors, and other trends in the external environment will help you do a better job of identifying possible market opportunities. A good place to start is with some background information. It will help to put the current situation in perspective.

BACKGROUND

Technological Change

The development of practical electronic computers in the 1950s marked the beginning of fundamental changes in the U.S. technological base. At first, the changes were slow—because computers were very expensive and very hard to use. For the computer to be useful, customers needed faster and easier ways to tell the computer what to do.

Computer companies realized that just making computers was not enough. They had to rethink their customers' needs—and their product. Computer experts turned their attention to developing good software—computer programs that could be used to solve problems. As better software was developed, the use of mainframe computers spread much more rapidly—especially among businesses.

Innovations in computer hardware and software continued. But the pace of change really picked up in the 1970s. Scientists invented new microchips and other electronic parts that made it possible to produce powerful and economical desktop computers. Companies like Apple Computer and Tandy Corporation (Radio Shack) saw the opportunity and entered the market with inexpensive microcomputers that were useful for both homes and businesses.

Derived Demand for Microcomputer Software

Computer cost was no longer a big problem—but software continued to be a limitation. There was not much software available for microcomputers. This started to change as growing demand attracted many firms to the market.

At first, the software firms were quite production oriented. A company could quickly develop a program and find many eager customers—even if the software did not meet their needs exactly. It seemed that any software was better than none.

The big breakthrough in software came when IBM introduced its personal computer. The IBM hardware was not that innovative. But there was a difference. Customers knew the IBM brand—and IBM made certain that software would be available. IBM developed some software itself. More important, however, IBM encouraged other firms to develop software that would work on its computers. In addition, other microcomputer producers who entered the market designed their computers to be IBM-compatible—so they could use the same software. This meant that there were more potential customers for a given type of software since it would work on different machines. Furthermore, because other hardware standards were in place, there was an opportunity for independent firms to develop and market improved hardware "add on" equipment—like disk drives and graphics adapters.

Market Growth and Competition

Competition among both hardware and software firms increased as the market grew. With more products available and few barriers to entry, effective market segmentation was often the best way to achieve a competitive advantage.   Software companies could avoid head-on competition by focusing on the needs of specific target markets—and developing marketing mixes to meet the needs of those customers.

Further, although the growth in the general market for desktop personal computers started to wane, new generations of technology in both hardware and software made it possible to add new hardware and software benefits specific to the needs of various market segments—and spark renewed sales. In some cases, the really innovative advances opened up new markets and resulted in new product life cycles.

For example, in the late 1980s and early 1990s advances in computer memory, processing speed, and disk storage made it possible to make computing easier—with operating systems, like Microsoft's Windows and IBM's OS/2, that take advantage of graphical user interfaces. During about the same period, miniaturization of electronic parts provided the impetus for small portable computers, such as IBM's popular notebooks and Apple's personal digital assistant, the Newton.

Just as these innovations were opening up new markets, other firms—like Novell and Lotus Development Corp.—were introducing hardware and software solutions to help people who work in groups to share information among their personal computers. Similarly, the early 1990s marked the introductory stage of multimedia computing—which blends full motion video, voice, pictures and other types of graphics, along with traditional text, numerical data, and computer control.

Despite the interest in multimedia computing, there were significant technical problems that limited its use—and its initial market acceptance. For example, the ideal of being able to incorporate full motion video segments and high quality audio in computer programs has been hampered by the amount of computer storage space and the processing speeds it required. Even a few minutes of full motion video (or CD quality music) could consume all of the storage space on a large hard disk. Some of these storage problems were partially overcome by specialized hardware and software "compression" procedures; here, the idea was to save multimedia data in a compressed format, and then expand it again when it was needed. Yet, video image quality was lost during these extra steps, which also added processing time of their own and further limited what could be done.

Another approach involved linking specialized storage media—like CD ROM disk drives and LaserDisc players—to the computer. Yet, none of these approaches worked very well—and they almost always required that the computer user be a real technical guru to make the pieces work together.

In spite of such problems, there were some focused successes. For example, producers of computers designed primarily for games were able to incorporate more realistic images, animation, and sound in their software. Similarly, some educational materials (like encyclopedias) that had in the past only been available in book form were able to incorporate limited multimedia elements by using CD ROM disks. Successes in areas like these showed that there was real interest—and significant market potential—if the problems of multimedia computing could be overcome.

This encouraged a great deal of effort to solving all the technical problems in this area. But, as computer producers worked on these problems, they were constantly reminded of the important lesson learned when IBM introduced its first personal computer: better multimedia hardware by itself would not be enough. Customers would need good multimedia software before they would be willing to buy an expensive new multimedia computer.

Cooperation among Software and Hardware Producers

This reality prompted computer producers and software firms to form partnerships—and work closely together. Microcomputer producers—even larger ones like IBM and Apple—shared ideas about their new machines with software producers so that programs would be available when new types of computers come on the market. The computer producers can't work with everybody—so each firm tends to focus on coordinating efforts with a set of software suppliers who have the ability to do a really good job. Developing quality software that works well requires a knowledge of the computer's details—and the success of the computer hinges on good software. It's that simple.

This background can give you important insights into the forces that led to the growth of your own company.

A NEW OPPORTUNITY

About four years ago, a company that had developed a good reputation with its reliable line of IBM-compatible laptop computers realized that many customers were unhappy with the poor performance of standard microcomputers when it came to any application involving multimedia. These customers said they were willing to buy a computer that was not from a major company—like IBM or Apple—if it really offered a "breakthrough" and made multimedia work well. For example, they wanted to be able to control the computer with voice commands or by touching symbols ("icons") on the screen—rather than by typing complex messages on the keyboard or by clicking a mouse. They wanted to be able to display high quality full motion video—like they were accustomed to from a VCR—on the computer screen. They also wanted to be able to easily incorporate sound effects—including voice messages and stereo music—in their computing work.

Once the most important customer needs were identified, the firm raised investment money to support the significant research and development effort needed to try to solve the problem. After several false starts, the technical folks came up with a real breakthrough—and the firm was able to obtain patents that gave it a virtual monopoly in producing a new generation multimedia computer. The firm also had the resources and the marketing strengths to market the computer it had in mind. But, the firm faced a big limitation. It did not have the skilled programmers to develop software that would take advantage of the new hardware—and thus really satisfy customers. Without software, the computer wouldn't sell.

A Solution to the Problem

This problem required a special solution. Many firms could develop useful software for the computer—and the computer maker wanted to encourage software development. But it was especially concerned about certain types of software—

software that just about every user would want. It was absolutely critical to have some high-quality software available when the computer was first introduced. And—to take full advantage of the new computer's features—the software developers would need to know details of the computer's design.

The computer producer turned to some small but skillful software firms and urged them to join in the effort of developing the product market for multimedia computing. Specifically, the computer firm agreed to provide the software developers with confidential information about the computer design—and promised to tell them about changes in its proprietary multimedia hardware before it introduced new models. In return for this information, a software company had to agree that it would focus full attention on software for the new computer.

Four software firms entered into such agreements with the computer company. Although the four software companies would be competing among themselves on equal terms, they alone would have the information (and technology license agreements) needed to develop certain types of software for this market. Other companies would be able to develop some general types of software—like wordprocessing programs. But several important types of software—such as programs for creating multimedia presentations—could only be developed by these four companies.

All of this planning and "partnering" paid off. Sales of the computer took off—even in the first year. Further, each of the four software companies introduced a successful software product. Your firm and the other three firms continue to grow and prosper as this multimedia specialty computer grows in popularity.

COMPETITORS IN A BROAD PRODUCT-MARKET

These four competitors are all focused on the same broad product-market. The broad product-market consists of businesses and final consumers in our country who have the special type of computer and who need software to handle their multimedia computing needs. While these firms are part of the overall software industry—they think of themselves as an industry since they alone compete in this product-market.

Each of the software firms has focused on multimedia software because it is one area where special knowledge of the computer's design limits further competition. In addition, almost everyone who buys and uses this type of computer wants and needs some sort of multimedia presentation software.

Since your firm is so heavily involved in this area, let's take a closer look at what needs are met by multimedia software.

Benefits Offered by Multimedia Software

With the right computer hardware support, multimedia software offers many powerful capabilities that translate to benefits for users. At one level, the software allows the user to capture and then play back—in whatever sequence is desired—any combination of full motion video, pictures, graphs, and audio tracks. For example, the software can "capture" (record) inputs from a video camera or VCR (such as home movies, product demonstrations, commercials) and edit, enhance, or combine them. In that regard, the software provides the user with many of the capabilities of a movie production studio—but at low cost. For example, an executive might use multimedia software to prepare a computer-aided presentation—for display on an large monitor or video beam projector. A home user might "freeze" one frame image from a video, add text to it, and print it on a color printer—for use as a greeting card. Or, a computer game could incorporate real scenes and people to add interest.

Such software also allows the user to "cut and paste" pictures and graphs and merge them together, perhaps with voice-over annotations. The right software makes it easy to experiment with different effects and approaches, and then "undo" any step that doesn't work as intended. New material may be added or deleted easily. The style or format of the multimedia materials can be changed quickly.

There are, however, some disadvantages to multimedia software. Some people still have trouble learning about the basic operation of a multimedia computer. For example, the software must be "trained" to recognize special voice commands from each user. Further, for many people, using multimedia computing is a really new idea and requires them to think in new ways. Thus, learning how to use specific multimedia software takes time—and may require special training. Even an experienced user can encounter problems. For example, with some software it's possible to accidentally press the wrong key and wipe out a carefully prepared multimedia sequence before it has been saved for later use. Further, the combined cost of a multimedia computer and software—and accessories such as color "scanners" and printers—is high.

Some customers compare these front-end costs (the investment in training and equipment) to the time and costs they can save later. For example, a company may be able to develop multimedia presentations that can then be used by many different sales people in the field—so they can save time preparing sales presentations and still do a better job during sales calls. Other customers are not trying to save money—they just want to learn and have fun.

Many users of the new computer think that the benefits of multimedia outweigh the limitations. In fact, many people use their computers primarily for one type or another of multimedia processing. As a result, demand for multimedia software is strong—and growth in the market is expected as more people learn about what it can do.

Product-Market Segments

In the beginning, no one was certain who would buy the special computer. So each software firm focused on designing a good general-purpose multimedia program that would take advantage of the computer's special features. After all, customers bought that computer because they wanted the special benefits it could offer. The software firms tried to develop one marketing mix that would do a pretty good job of meeting the needs of different market segments. This approach seemed to make sense in the beginning. It resulted in target markets that were large enough to be profitable. Now, however, problems are surfacing. All four firms offer pretty much the same thing. Although the number of potential customers has increased, competition is intense. There is a good opportunity to find profitable sub-markets.

Multimedia software produced by the four firms is purchased both by final consumers and by businesses. The variety of final users ranges from sophisticated commercial graphic artists to grade-school students. All of these potential customers are using the same computer equipment, but it is clear that some of their multimedia needs are different.

Market-Views' research reveals that most potential customers in the broad product-market can be classified into more homogeneous market segments. Market-Views has identified six main segments. Each segment has a nickname—to make it easier to remember. A description of each segment is provided below.

• The Modern Students

The *modern students* are college students who use multimedia to work on term projects and other school-related assignments. This is encouraged by colleges that have made multimedia instruction a high priority—in some cases even installing fiber optic "networks" in computer labs, dorms and classrooms so that multimedia materials are an important teaching and learning resource. Many of the modern students can't afford to buy a multimedia computer—but they can use one of the many available on campus. Even with access to a free computer, they want economical multimedia software of their own to access and use the multimedia resource materials available to them. Economy is a major concern for this segment. Students in this segment often form user groups to share advice and help each other solve software problems. Many campuses also have microcomputer support centers that answer questions about hardware and software. With so much help available, students don't seem to be particularly worried about learning to use software or about problems they might encounter. Modern students accounted for about 20 percent of multimedia sales last year. Multimedia is proving to be very popular on campuses—and this sub-market will probably continue to grow for some time.

• The Home Producers

The *home producers* segment contains a mix of households who use simple multimedia software to produce a variety of multimedia materials—everything from editing home movies to creating electronic "scrap books" of family pictures to producing home versions of MTV-like videos. In some homes, people even use the software to leave each other messages; for example, rather than just leave a list of things that need to be done, they quickly type the list and then "enhance it" with more detailed voice messages. Different members of the household may use the software for different reasons—but typically what they are doing is not very complicated given available technology. They're just having fun.

The home producers are pretty much on their own if they have a problem—so they prefer software that is easier to learn and less likely to result in a problem. Money for computer software usually must come from some other area of the household budget—so home producers have only limited interest in high-priced software. Last year, the home producers segment accounted for about 15 percent of total sales.

• The Harried Assistants

The *harried assistants* segment consists of secretaries, administrative assistants, and other employees who spend at least some of their time preparing and revising multimedia business presentations. For example, the boss may sketch out the ideas for what is to go in a multimedia presentation, then the assistant is expected to use the software to pull everything together into a polished looking presentation. Without special multimedia software, this would have been a massive headache, but with good software it's just becoming a normal part of the assistant's job. However, often the assistants are just learning about multimedia software—making the switch from preparing materials with a wordprocessor or desktop publishing program, or perhaps with a presentation graphics package. Thus, they want software that is not too hard to learn or use. Very quickly they must be able to use multimedia software to prepare many routine presentations. Moreover, one assistant often needs to satisfy requests from a number of different bosses—so the harried assistants need software that can handle a variety of multimedia needs. Most assistants worry about having difficulties with multimedia software. They seem to have good reason to worry; bosses who don't understand how multimedia works are not very understanding when there is a problem!

Although the assistants may influence the choice of a particular multimedia program—others in the company usually make the final purchase decision. In addition, companies often purchase a number of copies of the multimedia software—so that different assistants will be using the same program. Last year, sales to this segment amounted to approximately 25 percent of total sales.

• The Commercial Artists

The *commercial artists* segment consists of professional photographers, advertising agency creative people, package designers, and others who create and modify images and pictures for a living. Of all the segments, this group spends the most time using multimedia software. Commercial artists were often the innovators—among the first to use multimedia software. They use the multimedia software to create layouts and to compose images "on the fly"—perhaps with voice message annotation and notes about what they are trying to accomplish—and then they worry about final "polishing" later after they have initial feedback from a client. They are primarily concerned with speed and special commands for advanced image editing and formatting capabilities. The right multimedia software helps them to be more creative more quickly—and by saving them time and producing a better product they can improve their earnings. Sales to this segment accounted for about 10 percent of last year's total sales.

• The High-Tech Managers

High-tech managers buy multimedia software primarily for their own use at the office. They pick the brand of software they want—but the company pays for it. They often have a secretary or other assistant who does the routine work in developing a presentation (perhaps with some other compatible program)—so the managers use multimedia software less than most users. But they use computers for other parts of their work and want to be able to do some special types of multimedia themselves. For example, they might want to "whip out" a multimedia report—with fancy animated graphics and music—to highlight the results of a complex analysis; then the "report" is distributed to the computer screen of others in the company via electronic mail. Members of this segment are very interested in the number of capabilities offered. They take pride in the status of knowing about and using the very latest developments—and they don't want their colleagues to think they are just doing plain old multimedia work that a secretary could do. Thus, their choices when purchasing multimedia software are partially motivated by social needs for status and esteem. Last year, sales to this segment accounted for nearly 22 percent of the total.

• The Concerned Parents

The *concerned parents* are generally two-career professional couples with school-age children. These affluent—but busy—couples want to provide their kids with all of the advantages of multimedia learning; they see multimedia as an important trend for the future, and want to get their kids interested in it early. They also see multimedia computers and software as providing a valuable educational experience. They want simple software that children can learn and use themselves. Last year, the concerned parents accounted for 8 percent of total unit sales.

MARKET POTENTIAL

The Market Is Growing

The broad product-market appears to be in the middle part of the growth stage of the product life cycle. Industry experts think that growth in industry sales will continue for a number of years—perhaps for as much as a decade. Many experts believe that there is ample growth to fuel better profits for the whole industry—and for individual firms. However, even the optimists are unwilling to make precise forecasts too far into the future.

There is agreement, however, that the growth in market potential—what a whole segment might buy—will depend on several factors. These include the size of the segment, growth trends, the extent to which potential customers are aware of multimedia software and what it can do for them, and how well the marketing mix and customer service after the sale meets customers' needs.

Some Segments Are Growing Faster than Others

At present, the size of the various market segments differs substantially. Research found the harried assistants to be the largest segment with 25 percent of total unit sales last year. The concerned parents segment was the smallest with 8 percent. Current sales may provide a snapshot of the opportunity offered by each segment. However, sales to the different segments have grown at different rates. This can be seen in Exhibit 2A—which shows estimates of unit sales to each segment during the past three years. Of course, simply extending these trends could be dangerous—since factors behind the trends may change. In addition, these sales figures are estimates based on a marketing research survey of multimedia software users. Some people who responded to the survey couldn't recall exactly when they purchased the software—so it is best not to view these figures as exact.

Interpret Exhibit 2A with some caution. The large or fast-growing segments—in terms of unit sales—may not be the best targets. Some segments may prove to be more profitable than others—depending on how much it costs to develop a marketing mix that will meet their needs and depending on the price they will pay.

Advertising May Make More Customers Aware

Industry experts agree that the overall level and nature of industry advertising will affect market growth. Many customers still are unfamiliar with multimedia computers and software. Higher overall spending on advertising will help to inform more potential customers—and more of them are likely to enter the market. Because the life cycle is still in its growth stage, advertising so far has focused on building awareness and informing consumers about the product class. Advertising that helps pioneer the market may help your own firm—but it may also help competitors. On the other hand, competitive advertising focused on specific brands may increase a firm's share of the market now and in the future—but may do little to stimulate overall market growth.

Marketing Mix Must Meet Customers' Needs

It is important to emphasize that growth in the broad product-market—or in segments of the market—will depend on how well available marketing mixes meet customers' needs. At present, some customers are buying software that is not exactly what they want—they just purchase whatever comes closest to their ideal.

On the other hand, many customers will continue to wait—and not buy anything until the right product is available in the right place at the right price. Further, different segments have different needs. Thus, different marketing strategies—different marketing mixes for different target markets—may be required.

This last point is an important one—since the four firms in the market are at present all offering pretty much the same marketing mixes.

Exhibit 2A
Past Sales by Market Segment — Multimedia Software

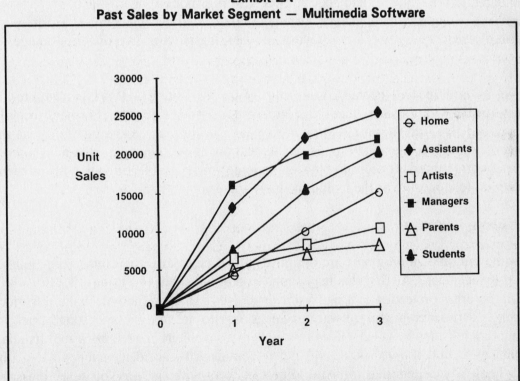

TYPICAL MARKETING MIXES

Product

There can be many technical differences in multimedia software. But research shows that most customers tend to simplify their evaluation process by grouping features into three main areas: (1) the number and variety of special commands, (2) protection against user errors, and (3) ease of learning.

• Special Commands

All multimedia programs offer many of the same basic commands. Standard commands allow the user to import or record video and audio signals, to respond to voice control, and to playback the multimedia elements alone or at the same time—for example in different "windows" on the computer screen. Standard editing commands also make it easy to rearrange, drop or add audio or video elements. Standard formatting commands allow the user to set the size of images on the screen and the timing between changes in screen displays. In addition to standard commands, a program may have a variety of more advanced or special commands. Examples of these include commands to add special effects to full motion video—such as "morphing" images (which changes an image into something different, as is often seen in movies), cutting out backgrounds, or merging parts of two different images into one.

Not all multimedia customers want a lot of special features. It doesn't help to have software with a feature that the customer doesn't want to use. Further, special features can also lead to errors—since accidentally using a command or using it in the wrong way may produce undesirable results that are hard to change. Even so, users in certain target markets seem to have an appetite for special features that allow them to have more control over their multimedia work.

• Error Protection

Some multimedia programs are designed to prevent users from doing something wrong by accident. At first this may sound good—but there is a trade-off. Software with more error protection is usually slower to use. An example will make this more concrete. Most multimedia software makes it easy to delete a picture, sound track, or segment of full motion video. This can be very convenient in revising a multimedia "document." But, if a user issues the delete command by accident much work can be lost. Thus, some users like software to protect them with an "are you sure" message (from the computer's speakers) when they issue the delete command. But that slows things down. An expert user just wants the program to make the change. All programs have some level of error protection. But, the extent of such error protection can vary substantially—and in total it affects how quickly you can use the software.

In short, some people like a lot of error protection—others prefer to do things faster.

• Ease of Learning

Another feature concerns how easy it is to learn to use the software. Some customers are worried about how long it will take to get going—and how much help is available if there is a problem. Different aspects of the product may address this concern. For example, some software companies provide a video tape tutorial along with the software—so the user can see how everything works. Others provide documentation that explains every detail of the commands and how to use them. Some also offer computerized tutorials or extensive on-line help systems that lead a novice through each step of using the software.

Not everyone is interested in all of this. In fact, some may see it as a problem. Very detailed documentation may slow down a knowledgeable user who wants a quick answer to a question. Computer tutorials are often paced too slowly and explain things the knowledgeable customer already knows. In addition, programs that are easy to learn are sometimes cumbersome to use. For example, programs that show a lot of instructions on the screen or provide audio explanations through the computer's speakers may make it easier to learn to use all the commands. But later, when the user knows the commands, it might be better to use the space on the screen to display the images that the user is manipulating, or to reserve the speakers for audio output.

• Product Modifications

Changes in technology as well as feedback and suggestions from customers mean that firms are continually doing research and development and updating and modifying their software products. In fact, all four firms in this market now have a yearly revision cycle. The start of each fiscal year brings announcements of new versions and releases of software in time for the dealer trade shows. In some instances, there may be major changes in the product features as firms attempt to better meet the needs of their target customers. In other cases only minor modifications are made to accommodate changes and additions to the computer hardware that runs the software. In general, large changes in a single year tend to significantly stress the R&D department and require use of expensive overtime or contract programmers.

As part of the license agreement with the producer of the multimedia computer, all four of the software firms must stick to the same basic standards for the format of the basic input and output files they create. Thus, multimedia files created by one software system can also be used on the software system offered by a different firm. Having a compatible file structure has helped the industry grow, but there is also a potential downside. Specifically, consumers who are considering upgrading to a new version of a software product may not be hesitant to switch to a competing software package—if it does a better job of meeting their needs. In other words, each firm in this market must constantly "earn" the loyalty of its customers.

Place

• Indirect Distribution

All four firms sell their software through middlemen who in turn sell direct to final customers. Some of the middlemen focus on sales to business customers, and some of them focus on sales to final consumers. Thus, in a technical sense, some of them are wholesalers and some of them are retailers. Regardless of their primary customer focus, they all refer to themselves as dealers.

• Dual Distribution

All four firms currently use dual channels of distribution to reach customers. The two channels involve different types of dealers. The different dealers tend to attract different types of customers.

• Full Service Dealers (Channel 1)

The dealers in one channel typically serve local customers with a limited line of computers and computer software that they carry in stock. Some sell only software. But all of these dealers have well-trained salespeople who provide customers with technical information, demonstrations, and personalized service. These middlemen are also attractive to customers who want to be able to see and compare different products—and to customers who want the assurance of having the supplier nearby in case of problems.

Originally, these dealers were the only way for a software producer to get to the target market. Thus, for convenience we will refer to this as Channel 1. These dealers were willing to handle multimedia software because it was new and gave them a product that was distinctive relative to what was available from mail-order discounters—who were mainly interested in carrying software that was already popular and would turnover fast, even without much personal selling effort.

• Discount Dealers (Channel 2)

However, as the market for multimedia software grew, the mail-order discount dealers became more interested in carrying the product. The dealers in this channel (Channel 2) offer more limited service and handle larger assortments of products. They also offer lower prices. These discounters often rely on mail, telephone, or fax orders for the bulk of their business. These dealers are mainly order-takers—they don't provide much service or help to customers. Rather, they primarily appeal to price-sensitive customers as well as to customers who don't have a local supplier with the right selection.

• Distribution Intensity

At present, producers of multimedia software are in general not attempting to obtain intensive distribution (i.e., making their products available through all suitable and available dealers) in either channel. Rather, it appears that your firm and competitors are trying to sell through about 30 percent of the available dealers in each channel. When multimedia software was first introduced, the best dealers were not willing to carry it unless the producers provided exclusive distribution agreements—at least for a two year introductory period. Some other dealers didn't want to handle the software at all because the sales volume was initially low. Now that the market is growing, however, more dealers are interested in handling the product. Further, having the software more widely available might increase sales and market share—in part because it is more conveniently available to more customers and in part because of the extra promotional push from dealers. On the other hand, there's no "free lunch" when it comes to increasing distribution intensity. In particular, dealers may pay less attention to a product if it is available from many other competing dealers; further, it takes more promotion effort—especially time from sales reps. Trade promotion may also be an issue. Specifically, if firms in the industry start to use trade promotion—and dealers start to expect it—more promotion spending may be required to keep a larger number of dealers happy and active in selling a particular brand of software.

In short, the dealers in the two channels provide different marketing functions and appeal to different types of customers. The different types of dealers also require different kinds of promotional attention from the software producers.

Promotion

Promotion blends in the multimedia software business include sales promotion, personal selling, and advertising. In addition, firms try to get publicity in computer magazines and other trade publications, and they try to encourage good word of mouth communication (endorsements) among consumers. Software producers target most of their advertising toward final customers; personal selling and sales (trade) promotion focus on the dealers.

• Personal Selling

Personal selling is important to software producers. Each firm maintains its own staff of trained sales representatives. These salespeople sell to the dealers who in turn sell to the final customer. To better serve the needs of the different dealers, the sales force is organized by channel. Thus, any one salesperson works either with the traditional dealers or with mail-order discount dealers—but not both.

Sales representatives service current accounts and develop new ones. This requires a mix of selling and supporting tasks. Selling involves getting orders from current dealers and developing new accounts. It also includes efforts to persuade dealers to put more emphasis on pushing the firm's software. By contrast, supporting tasks include explaining technical details, training the dealer's sales staff, and keeping the dealers up to date on new developments—including changes in sales promotion deals available from the software firm.

The percent of personal selling effort spent on support activities tends to vary with the amount of service that the dealers provide to their customers. Dealers that provide a lot of service and selling help to their customers look for support and training from the software producers whose products they sell.

• Advertising

Software producers advertise in many media—trade and computer magazines, publications such as *The Wall Street Journal, Time,* and *Newsweek,* and even on television. Last year advertising expenditures by the four producers totaled $1 million, or an average of $250,000 per firm. Firms use various types of advertising depending on their objectives. These types may be grouped into the five categories summarized below:

1. *Pioneering advertising* works to build primary demand—or demand for the whole product category—rather than promoting a specific brand. In the past, this was an important type of advertising since consumers needed to become aware of the possibilities of multimedia software. Even now, a very substantial untapped market of consumers do not know about multimedia or what it involves.

2. *Direct competitive advertising* attempts to build selective demand for a firm's own brand. Its main objective is immediate buying action, with relatively less carryover to future years.

3. *Indirect competitive advertising* also attempts to build selective demand, but it tends to focus on influencing *future* purchases—so that when a customer is ready to buy, he or she will chose that brand.

4. *Reminder advertising* reinforces earlier promotion and merely tries to keep the brand's name before the consumer. It doesn't do much good if customers are not already familiar with the brand, but it can be quite efficient if the brand is already well known.

5. *Corporate (institutional) advertising* focuses on promoting the overall firm rather than a specific product. Corporate advertising is commonly used by firms with multiple products—as a way to build interest in all of the products at lower cost.

• Sales Promotion

Sales promotion is a relatively new tool for the multimedia software producers. In fact, so far each of the four software firms has turned to outside specialists to help plan sales promotions.

Dealers are the target of most of the sales promotion—which includes trade show presentations, special brochures, dealer sales contests, and a variety of deals to the trade. Deals seem to be quite popular. For example, a producer might offer a dealer additional products free with a purchase of a certain quantity.

The objective of these trade promotions is to encourage the dealer to carry and push a particular brand or to devote special attention to selling it. This has caused some concern among the producers. Some think that sales promotion simply increases each firm's costs. They think that a firm that doesn't do the promotion will lose market share—but that no one gains if everyone is offering basically the same types of promotion. In other words, promotions seem to impact a firm's market share—positively if it is the only firm running a promotion or negatively if it is the only firm without a promotion. However, no one seems to gain much if everone offering promotions.

Because the firms in this market have not been using sales promotion very long, it's too early to know if these concerns are valid. But sales promotion is often more effective in prompting short-term responses than in building longer-term brand insistence.

• Publicity and Word of Mouth

Multimedia software firms in the industry have in general enjoyed favorable publicity—primarily coverage in computer magazines read by both dealers and final consumers. In general, the magazines provide reviews of new releases of the software, and tout the advantages of whatever is different. Thus, the general effect of publicity has been favorable for the industry.

However, in recent years a major consumer publication has published annual ratings of the help that multimedia software users were able to get from software producers' customer service telephone lines. Unfortunately, the news has not been all good, and it may even have hurt sales. One year, when several companies' customer service support did not keep pace with the growth in sales, negative magazine ratings and negative word-of-mouth among consumers resulted in shifts in market share toward companies that were offering the best customer service. In response to all of this, the companies that had earned the weaker customer service ratings increased their spending on customer service, and now there is not much difference among firms in the industry with respect to the after-the-sale customer service that they provide.

Customer service must be carefully managed; at a minimum the ratings published by computer the magazine call attention to firms that don't provide adequate service—and on a more positive note superior customer service probably translates to some increase in market share. On the other hand, the cost of providing customer service—like other expenses—must be covered in the price a software firm charges.

Price

Suggested retail list prices for multimedia software have ranged from $150 to $400 depending on the features of the software, the manufacturer, and the channel(s) in which it is distributed.

The software producer decides on a wholesale price at which to sell software to the dealers. The dealers then decide what retail price to charge their customers. Thus, the producer can't actually control the price to the final customer. But this is not a significant problem. Dealers tend to stick to the same price-setting approaches. Thus, the producer can get a pretty good idea what the price will be at the end of the channel.

• Dealers Set the Retail Price

Dealers typically set the retail price by using a customary markup percent. The markup percent is different in the two channels. The difference is due to differences in the amount of service provided by the dealers and differences in the quantities they sell. The customary markup by dealers in channel 1 is 50 percent. Dealers in Channel 2 use a 35 percent markup. The formula for the markup percent is:

$$\text{Dealer markup percent} = \frac{\text{(Retail selling price} - \text{Wholesale price)}}{\text{Retail selling price}}$$

Note that these dealers figure markup percents are based on the *retail* selling price.

While the middlemen in the two channels rely on standard markups to determine their selling price, pricing by the software producers must be based on consideration of their costs and on estimates of the demand curve. There are several reasons why producers can't use a standard markup percent. First, costs of producing the actual software and documentation are small compared to the costs of product development. Second, the most profitable quantity may not be what would sell at a price based on a standard markup percent.

The software producers do announce a suggested retail price. Dealers are not obligated to sell the software at that price, but it may be difficult for them to ask for more than that amount. However, they can quite easily charge a lower price. In fact, price-cutting is common among the discount mail-order houses. This is reflected in their lower markup percent.

The discounters may cut the price even further if they have been offered a sales promotion deal of some sort by a producer. In effect, some of these deals lower the dealer's cost per product. In the discount channel, the dealers tend to pass along some of the savings to customers—in the form of a lower retail price. By contrast, most traditional dealers just view a deal from the producer as a way to make a higher profit per unit.

• Customer Price Perceptions

Consumer research suggests that most multimedia software customers have in mind a reference price—the retail price they expect to pay for their software. However, different software users tend to look at the retail price in different ways—and the reference price is not the same for everybody. Some people think that the price indicates the quality of the software—and for them a higher reference price is better; they interpret a low price as a signal of low quality. Others believe that the price has little to do with the actual quality. Instead, they think of quality in terms of what fits their needs. And if they have a low reference price, a low price on the software is part of what will meet their needs.

CUSTOMER CHOICES AMONG BRANDS

It's difficult to pinpoint why some customers respond favorably to a marketing mix and others don't. But understanding the needs of the different segments and then seeing the different marketing mix possibilities will provide some insights. Customers do look for products that have the features they want at the right price. But other factors also motivate purchase of a particular brand of software.

The amount of attention that a dealer devotes to the brand may make a difference too. Some customers are uncertain about what they want or may not know very much about the different brands available. A dealer's salesperson who is knowledgeable about a particular brand and able to demonstrate its features may be the deciding factor in completing the sale. Furthermore, some customers prefer to buy from the traditional dealers—and others prefer the discounters. A customer is more likely to buy a brand that is available from a preferred type of dealer.

Brand awareness is important too. Advertising helps make customers aware of a brand. A customer may insist on a familiar brand—but be indifferent to one that is unfamiliar.

CONCLUSION

This report reviews the current state of the broad market in which you compete. It explains how your firm got to where it is today. It discusses the nature of the competition you face. It also highlights a number of potential opportunities—by identifying more homogeneous market segments and providing information that may help in developing better marketing mixes to meet the needs of the target market.

As consultants, we have tried to provide an objective report. We have avoided the temptation to inject much personal opinion—but rather have focused on the facts. In closing, however, we have a few recommendations to share.

We think that you, as the new marketing manager, have a real opportunity to do a better job than your predecessor did in selecting a target market and blending the 4Ps. The current head-to-head competition gives no one a competitive advantage. It appears that each competitor has pretty much followed the others. No firm seems to be doing an especially effective job of meeting the needs of specific targets.

It may also be time to take a broader look at the product-market. Your firm now has a single product. There may be an opportunity to expand your product line to better meet the needs of the target market. In addition, your arrangement with the computer producer allows you to develop a product that most other suppliers can't offer. Of course, you might face competition from your three primary competitors who have similar arrangements with the computer maker. But, even so, that is less competition than many software producers face. Of course, significant resources will be needed for your firm to develop any additional product—so any decision in that area will certainly need the approval of the firm's president.

We hope that this report has been helpful. We wish you the best of success with your new responsibilities. If Market-Views, Inc. can be of further assistance in the future, please call on us.

3
Marketing Department Responsibilities

Note: Before the previous marketing manager retired, the president asked him to summarize the marketing department's responsibilities—and review other relevant information that might be helpful to a new marketing manager. This chapter is the text of the memorandum prepared by the previous marketing manager.

INTRODUCTION

As marketing manager, you are in charge of planning marketing activities, implementing your plans, and controlling them. You play an important role in strategic planning—because you are heavily involved in matching the firm's resources to its market opportunities.

Much of your time will be spent developing a marketing plan. So this memo focuses on strategy decision areas that need to be included in your plan. But it also deals with implementing and controlling the plans you make. Objectives should set the course of your planning, so that is a good place to start.

OBJECTIVES

Your basic objectives are to use the resources of the firm wisely to meet target customer needs and contribute to the firm's profit. The time period is important here. Building long-term profitability sometimes requires that you spend money that results in lower short-term profits—or even losses. This does not mean that you can take losses lightly. Ultimately, the firm must earn profits to survive. And, if other competing firms continually earn higher profits, it may be difficult to attract investors and the resources the firm needs.

These objectives are general. You will want to set other, more specific objectives. That way, you will know when your marketing strategy is on course—or if it needs to be changed.

Your objectives should be realistic. The firm does not have unlimited resources—and it doesn't make sense for the marketing department to develop a plan that requires money the firm doesn't have.

RESOURCES

The firm has many talented employees. This is important to you. It means that the software programmers can develop the products you think will meet customers' needs. The firm also has the equipment and facilities to produce and distribute the products. But there are limits to these resources—and how much you can spend on a marketing strategy.

To make certain that there is enough money to operate the firm, the president sets a budget for each department for each year. You get your budget before you develop your marketing plan for the next year.

The president has more money to spend when profits are good. So a successful marketing strategy will lead to a higher budget. But, don't expect the president to give you a budget equal to all of the profit you generate; after all, other areas need budgets too. Further, the president knows that you need enough money to do a good job even if profits have been down. In fact, the firm gets data from a trade association on marketing spending by competing firms. The president analyzes this data—to be certain that you get a large enough budget to develop a competitive strategy. In general, I recommend that you spend the budget that is allocated to you. If you use the money wisely, you should be able to leverage your spending into even greater revenue. But, don't spend foolishly just to use up the money; remember that expenses must be paid before profits start to accumulate!

Once in the past, the marketing department appealed to the president to increase the budget amount—because we thought we had a sensible way to spend the money. At that time, the president did not grant our request, but he said that he did appreciate the accompanying proposal that explained how we wanted to spend the money and the results expected. The president's memo indicated that he would take the budget matter under consideration and that we would be told if there was enough money to entertain special budget requests. The memo also said that the president was giving consideration to authorizing a discretionary reserve fund. If the president authorizes a reserve fund, you would be able to spend against that fund, save it to spend in a later period, or simply leave it for an emergency. At any rate, the president will let you know if anything changes on the budget front. Unless you hear something different, you should manage your spending so that it doesn't exceed your budget.

The firm has developed planning forms (and decision support software) that make this easy. Although budget planning is not difficult, it is important. Thus, additional information about specific budget expenses is given later in this memo.

Remember that a smart strategy need not be a high-cost strategy. Some target markets can be served well even with a low-cost marketing mix. Others might require a costly marketing mix but still be profitable. The focus of the marketing department is not on the budget per se—but rather matching the available resources to market opportunities. That requires careful selection of target markets—and skillful blending of the marketing mix. You will be able to do a better job in these areas if you know the strategy decision areas over which you have control.

PRODUCT

The firm already has an established product—and a completely new product can't be developed and marketed without the president's authorization. But that doesn't mean that you can't modify the firm's established product to better meet the needs of target customers.

As marketing manager, you decide when and how product features should change. These decisions should be based on information about target market needs, costs of the features, and costs of changing those features. Obviously, what competitors are offering in the market is also relevant.

Features

You make decisions about three features that customers consider important: the number of special commands, the level of error protection, and the ease of learning. After you specify the features, the R&D people take over to create the product.

But there are limits. Computer limitations prevent software developers from creating software with more than 20 special commands. And no one wants software with fewer than five special commands. The software industry uses a standard rating for levels of error protection. The rating can be between 1 and 10—where 1 is very low on error protection and 10 is high. Similarly, there is an accepted 1 to 10 industry rating for ease of learning. Thus, you specify the features of your product by deciding on the number of special commands (between 5 and 20) and the ratings (from 1 to 10) for the level of error protection and ease of learning.

Cost of R&D for Product Modification

The research and development people can in general modify the product quite quickly, within the limits discussed above. Further, experience shows that the number of special commands and the level of error protection can be *decreased without cost*. But the cost of other R&D product modifications can be substantial—especially if large changes are required in a single planning period. Further, these R&D and new product development costs are charged to the marketing budget—so they must be considered in developing the marketing plan.

The cost accounting experts in the firm have provided some help here. They have figured out a simple and accurate way to estimate the R&D cost of modifying each feature. Their approach is summarized in the table below:

Estimating the Costs of R&D for Product Modifications

FEATURE	Feasible Range	Cost to Change Level from Previous Period	
		To Decrease Level	To Increase Level
Special Commands	5-20	no cost	$8,000 × (change) × (change)
Error Protection	1-10	no cost	$5,000 × (change) × (change)
Ease of Learning	1-10	$3,000 × (change)	$3,000 × (change) × (change)

In this table, the term *change* refers to the difference in the level of the feature from one period to the next. The total product modification cost is the sum of the costs to change individual features.

Let's consider an example. The table below shows the costs to modify a brand which in the previous period had 6 special commands, an error protection rating of 4, and an ease of use rating of 3 to create a "new" brand with 8 special commands, an error protection rating of 3, and an ease of learning rating of 5.

Example of R&D Product Modification Costs

FEATURE	LEVEL Old Brand	LEVEL New Brand	CHANGE	COST
Special Commands	6	8	+2	$8,000 x 2 x 2 = $32,000
Error Protection	4	3	-1	no cost for decrease = $0
Ease of Learning	3	5	+2	$3,000 x 2 x 2 = $12,000

Thus, to made the changes described above the total product modification cost would be $32,000 + $0 + $12,000 = $44,000.

Note that it costs more if R&D must make big changes in a short period of time. For example, to increase the number of Special Commands from 6 to 10 in a single period would be $8,000 x 4 x 4 = $128,000. By contrast, to increase from 6 to 8 in one period and then increase from 8 to 10 in the following period would only be $64,000 (i.e., as shown in the table above, $32,000 for each period). Thus, it is wise to consider whether the added R&D costs to make really big changes in a short period of time are really justified, or if planning incremental changes over a longer period may make sense. Unfortunately, there are no easy answers in this area. Sometimes the advantages of speed in giving the market what it wants justifies the expense, but that may depend on what kinds of changes competitors make, and how fast they make them.

Regardless of how big a product change you want to make, the cost of the R&D for the required product modification is charged to your budget in the period when the changes are made. Further, the total product modification cost stays the same regardless of how much you sell in that period. If the product is not changed in the next period, there is no product modification cost for that period.

You can modify your brand again in future years if that is necessary to implement your strategy. However, product modification costs occur each time you change the product—even if the features are returned to the level of a previous year. For example, you might reduce the number of special commands one year and then add them back the next year. Although the total number of commands would be the same, there would be a cost to modify the software to include the commands again.

All product modifications are completed before production for the year starts. Thus, all units sold during the period have the new features. This is another reason why it is so important to have your plan in by the deadline specified by the president. If the plan is late, there may not be time to modify the product before production must begin.

Unit Production Cost

The production department reports that the level on each feature directly affects the unit production cost. Specifically,

Unit production cost = $4 x (Number of special commands)
+ $3 x (Error protection rating)
+ $2 x (Ease of learning rating).

Thus, your unit cost can vary from $25 to $130 depending on the features of the brand. The cost of producing units is not charged to the marketing department budget. But cost is certainly an important consideration. A product that is costly to produce may require a price that is too high for the target market. And customers may not want—or buy—a product with the wrong combination of features. Further, the cost of goods sold for the period—along with other expenses—is subtracted from sales revenue to arrive at profit contribution.

Experts in the production department have been studying ways to reduce production costs. In a draft report, they suggested that they may be able to achieve some economies of scale as the firm's cumulative production quantity increases. Specifically, they estimated that they should be able to reduce unit production costs by about 3 percent for each additional 100,000 units the firm produces. However, these potential cost savings are dependent on making changes in the equipment used by the production department, and the v.p. of production and the v.p. of finance are still debating the wisdom of purchasing the equipment. However, the president will make an announcement if the equipment is purchased. Unless there is such an announcement, you should continue to use the unit cost estimates overviewed above.

Customer Service

While our basic product is the software we sell, many customers expect to be able to get after-the-sale customer service if they have a question. They think of the availablility of technical help as part of the product they buy. So customer service seems to be an important issue. And the service level a firm provides is getting more attention in the press. Firms that haven't handled it well have faced bad publicity and a backlash in sales.

As is the practice of our competitors, we leave it to the customer to pay for the phone call to ask a question—so telephone line charges are not an expense. But the marketing department must decide how much money to spend on staff to support the customer service telephone lines.

It appears that most customer service calls come from new customers—within the first year after they have purchased our software. And for the most part the questions are easy to answer. Thus, we have been able to staff the phones with parttime employees whom we schedule to work when the calls are heaviest; they can always turn the tough questions—or the real problems—over to one of the programmers.

At any rate, the money spent to support customer service comes out of the marketing department budget. It makes sense to take a careful look at spending in this area. A mistake may certainly hurt us; it's not clear whether doing a really good job can help us.

PLACE

In developing your marketing plan, you must decide on the level of distribution intensity that you want in each channel of distribution. Operationally, you can think of distribution intensity as the percentage of available dealers in each channel that you want to stock and sell your software.

In an absolute sense, the level of distribution intensity (market exposure) in a channel may range from exclusive to selective to intensive—depending on your firm's marketing strategy. Exclusive distribution is selling through only one dealer in each area—and implies that you would expect sales people to call on a relatively small percentage of the available dealers in a channel. Selective distribution is selling through those dealers who will give your product special attention; it implies that the sales reps may call on a mid-range percentage of the available dealers in a channel. And intensive distribution is selling through all responsible and suitable dealers in a channel, although as a practical matter it may be difficult and expensive to achieve 100 percent coverage.

Because the dealers in the two channels are quite different, the level of distribution intensity in one channel has no direct influence on the level of distribution intensity in the other. Therefore you may want different levels of distribution intensity in the different channels. In fact, if you wish you can elect to stop selling in one of the channels. We've considered that in the past, but so far have not had time to study whether it might be a good idea.

In your marketing plan, use a rating of 0 (i.e., zero percent of the dealers) if you don't want to use dealers in a certain channel at all. Otherwise, use a rating between the extremes of 1 percent of the dealers (the most exclusive) and 100 percent of the dealers (the most intensive) to indicate the distribution intensity level you desire. Because this "percentage of dealers" approach has been used in the firm for some time now, it is a concise way to summarize what type of distribution you're planning.

PROMOTION

Personal Selling

The sales force plays a key role in recruiting new dealers, getting orders from dealers, and providing them with support and training. Because of differences in dealers, sales reps specialize by channel.

The marketing manager is responsible for deciding how many sales reps the firm needs in total—and how many are assigned to each channel. This is an important market strategy decision area. Decisions here must consider the distribution intensity level in each channel. Implementing intensive distribution requires more personal selling effort—more sales reps—than selective distribution. Similarly, selective distribution requires more sales reps than exclusive distribution. Too little sales coverage in channels will hurt sales and relations with dealers. Too much coverage doesn't help sales—but it does add to sales force costs and therefore to overall marketing costs.

Personal selling salaries—$20,000 a year per rep—are charged to the marketing budget. Each sales rep also earns 5 percent commission on all sales to dealers. Since the total commission amount varies with the quantity sold, sales commissions are not paid out of the marketing department budget. But they are an expense so they directly affect contribution to profit.

The commission percent is currently set by company policy—to keep sales compensation in line with pay for other jobs in the company. However, the director of the Human Resources department has acknowledged that the marketing department might be better able to better motivate the sales reps if it could set the commission rate. We had a meeting with the president on this issue, and it is being considered. I assume that the president will let you know if marketing area responsibility in this area is to be expanded.

New sales reps can be hired as needed to expand the sales force. Beyond the $20,000 a year salary, there is no direct charge for hiring a new rep. However, in this company new reps spend about 20 percent of the first year in training. So, in the first year, they are only 80 percent as productive as an experienced rep.

You can fire sales reps (but not all of them) if you want to reduce the size of the sales force. But you must make firing decisions carefully. It disrupts a rep's life to lose his or her job. Furthermore, the company gives each fired rep $5,000 in severance pay, and the $5,000 must be paid from the marketing department budget.

Sometimes you can avoid hiring or firing by reassigning a rep from one channel to the other. There is no cost to reassign a rep. And because experienced reps seem to adjust to the new channel situation quickly, there is no real loss in selling effectiveness.

The president of our firm feels very strongly that sales reps play an important role in developing good long-term relations with dealers. To ensure good relations with dealers, the president has instructed that sales reps spend 10 percent of their time on non-selling or support activities. These activities include explaining the technical details of the product, training the dealers' salespeople, and generally building goodwill with the dealers. Clearly, firms that have ignored these support activities in the past have lost important dealers. Even so, it's hard to tell if 10 percent is the right allocation for support tasks.

Advertising

Advertising is used to inform customers about multimedia software in general. It's also used to promote the features of the firm's brand relative to competing brands. How much to spend on advertising is an important strategy decision. Advertising costs are paid from the marketing budget. The firm works with an advertising agency that helps develop the actual ads and works out the details of what media to use.

The ad agency argues that how much you spend on advertising impacts advertising effectiveness. However, the ad agency cannot say exactly how large a sales volume will result from a given advertising budget. This is because customers respond to the whole marketing mix, not just advertising. But the ad agency has provided some general guidelines.

First, advertising impact depends not only on your firm's level of advertising but also on what competitors spend on advertising. Very low levels of advertising—below some threshold level—will have little impact. The advertising message will be lost among the clutter of competitors' ads. But, at the other extreme, there is an upper limit on the sales that advertising can generate. Money spent on advertising that approaches or exceeds that saturation level is wasted.

Advertising has the greatest effect in the year it's done. But some benefit may carryover to the next year or future years. Advertising impact may also vary depending on the type of advertising that's done. The agency works with the firm to select the best type of advertising for the money available. Marketing department decisions in that area are usually based on what competitors are doing and on the stage in the product life cycle, as well as the objectives to be accomplished.

PRICE

Legal Environment

Price is an important strategy decision area. You set the wholesale price—the price paid by your dealers. At present, the legal department in the firm requires that you charge all dealers the same price. However, the firm's lawyers are studying the laws in this area. They think that it may be legal to charge a different wholesale price to dealers in the two channels since they provide different kinds of marketing functions. Until the lawyers decide, however, you must charge the same wholesale price in each channel.

Price Affects Demand

Dealers set the retail price—but you should consider the likely retail price when you set the wholesale price. The retail price will affect the quantity demanded by the target market. Some segments of the market are more price-sensitive than others.

You can easily calculate the likely retail price because dealers use customary markup percents—50 percent in Channel 1 and 35 percent in Channel 2. The way to do the calculation is:

$$\text{(Likely) retail price} = \frac{\text{Wholesale Price} \times 100}{(100 - \text{Markup percent})}$$

You are free to change the wholesale price from one year to the next. But substantial price changes from year to year may confuse customers and dealers.

Price Should Cover Costs

The revenue you earn is equal to the wholesale price times the quantity sold. The price should be high enough to cover unit production costs and leave enough to contribute to other expenses (including sales commissions) and profit. Planning is important here.

As discussed earlier, you can estimate unit production costs based on the product features you're planning. Other costs to consider are those that are charged to the marketing department budget. Most of these have been covered earlier. As a convenient summary, however, they are listed below:

Product modification costs (if any),
Customer service costs
Sales force salaries and severance pay,
Advertising expense, and
Marketing research expense.

Marketing research expense depends on how many marketing research reports you buy. Marketing research is covered next.

MARKETING RESEARCH

Marketing research can be an important source of information about your target market, how well your marketing plan is working, and what competitors are doing. Some marketing research information is available free from secondary sources and from the firm's marketing information system (MIS). In addition, an outside marketing research firm sells a variety of useful marketing research reports. Examples of the different reports are provided in the next chapter, but they are briefly described below.

Information Available at No Cost

• Industry Sales Report

Each year, the industry trade association compiles an Industry Sales Report and provides a copy to each firm in the industry. The report summarizes the total unit sales and the total (retail) dollar sales for each brand. It also reports the market shares for each firm based on both unit sales and dollars sales. Moreover, it gives total unit sales and total (retail) dollars sales for each distribution channel.

• Product Features and Prices Report

Sales reps are instructed to report back to the firm the features of all brands on the market and the retail price for each brand in each channel. This information is organized in the firm's marketing information system and is summarized at the end of the year in a Product Features and Prices Report.

• Marketing Activity Report

Over time, the market research department collects information about each competitor's promotion blend. Competitors try to keep their plans secret—so it's impossible to get this information in advance. However, much of it is quickly available from advertising media and trade associations, dealers, trade publications, and even competitors' reports to stockholders. This information is compiled in the firm's MIS to produce the Marketing Activity Report. It includes summaries—for each firm—of spending on advertising, sales force size and commission rate, and any sales promotion activity. This timely information is fairly accurate and thus gives an idea of what competitors are doing in the market.

Reports from an Outside Marketing Research Firm

An outside marketing research firm specializes in ongoing studies of the software market in which you compete. Results from its studies are summarized in six reports. The reports are available each year. But the marketing research firm requires advance payment. You can purchase any report or combination of reports. The costs for the different reports vary. The title of each report and its cost is listed in the table below. A brief description of each report follows—and samples appear in the next chapter.

Costs of Marketing Research Reports

Report Number	Title of Report	Cost
1	Market Share by Segment (all brands)	$15,000
2	Market Share by Channel (all brands)	$12,000
3	Consumer Preference Study	$30,000
4	Marketing Effectiveness Study	$25,000
5	Sales by Segment by Channel (firm's brand)	$15,000
6	Customer Shopping Habits Survey	$7,000

• Market Share by Segment

This report gives the market shares (based on units sold) for each brand in each market segment. It also gives the total unit sales for each segment.

• Market Share by Channel

This report summarizes the market shares, based on units sold, for each brand in each distribution channel. The report also includes total unit sales for each channel.

• Consumer Preference Study

This study summarizes the results of a sample survey of actual and potential customers from the various market segments. Customers indicate their most preferred (or ideal) level for each product feature. The numbers in the report are the average values reported by members of each segment.

Although representative customers are surveyed, the sample estimates may not be exact for the whole population. The research firm says that the results are accurate to within 10 percent of the true values for the different market segments.

This report also gives a price range for each segment. This range merely indicates the prices that members of the different segments typically expect to pay for multimedia software.

• Marketing Effectiveness Report

This report summarizes the results of survey research on the effectiveness of your customer service as well as your advertising and personal selling decisions—both in an absolute sense and relative to competitors.

One measure of advertising effectiveness is the proportion of customers who are aware of your brand. This measure is reported as a Brand Awareness index ranging from 0.0 to 1.0. A higher index indicates greater awareness (familiarity). In practice, however, an index greater than .9 is very rare.

There is also a measure based on the customer service the firm provides. It is reported as a percentage rating, where a lower percentage suggests lower satisfaction with the service provided. This firm-specific measure can be compared with a measure of the average rating for the overall industry, which is also provided.

Additional indices indicate the effectiveness of the firm's efforts in each of the channels of distribution. The marketing research firm develops the Sales Rep Workload index by studying how sales reps spend their time and how well satisfied dealers are with the service they receive from a rep. An index of less than 100 percent indicates that sales reps can satisfactorily handle all their accounts and could potentially call on more dealers. On the other hand, an index that exceeds 100 percent indicates that sales reps are overloaded and trying to call on more dealers than they can effectively service.

The Dealer Satisfaction index is basically a summary measure of what dealers think about the quality and effectiveness of your sales force as well as any trade promotion assistance they receive. This index generally varies above and below 1.00. If it is less that 1.00, it suggests that dealers are not satisfied with some aspects of your promotion blend, at least relative to what competitors are doing. If it is greater than 1.00, this may be an area of competitive advantage. However, this advantage may be coming at the cost of greater spending on sales effort or promotion in the channel.

The Channel Strength ("Push") index is basically a summary measure of the overall "push" that your brand gets in consumer purchases decisions from dealers in the channel of distribution. It takes into consideration the number of dealers who are carrying your brand and how much effort they are willing to put behind it—relative to competing brands. Like the Brand Awareness index, the values on this index range between 0.0 and 1.00; however, in practice values over .80 are rare.

The research firm will not sell all of this detailed information for competing brands. But the report does provide some summary information. It gives the number of competitors with a lower index and the number of competitors with an index that is the same or greater. This report is expensive—but it does provide insights about your marketing strengths and weaknesses.

• Detailed Sales Analysis

This report details the number of units of your brand sold to each market segment through each channel. It can be very useful to see if the intended target market is buying the product—and, if so, from what dealers.

• Customer Shopping Habits

This study reports the results of survey research to determine the percentage of time that customers in the different segments shop in Channel 1 compared with Channel 2. The research is based on a sample of customers, and because of "sampling error" the results may not be exact for the whole population of customers. However, the market research firm says that the sample estimates are within 5 percent of the true values for the full population of customers.

Marketing Research—Benefits versus Costs

Much useful market research information is available. You should weigh the potential benefits of this information against the cost. Before deciding to buy a report, think about how you will use the information. Further, think about how the information can be used in combination with other data to give you additional insights. Advance planning for marketing research can lead to a more sensible use of your marketing budget.

FORECASTING DEMAND

It is the responsibility of the marketing department to forecast demand for the coming year. This forecast may be based on many different kinds of information—past sales trends, estimates of target market potential and growth, juries of executive judgment (for example, about what competitors are likely to do), and market research about customers' preferences. Of course, the forecast must consider how well the marketing mix meets target customers' needs.

Developing a good forecast is important for several reasons. You will need a forecast of what you expect to sell to evaluate your marketing plan—to estimate expected revenues and profit/contribution. But there is an even more immediate reason. The production department uses the estimate of demand as a production order quantity. This is an important decision for marketing management.

The Production Order Quantity

Lead times to produce software are short. As a result, the production department is able to increase production as much as 20 percent above your production order quantity to satisfy unexpected demand. It can also reduce the actual production quantity by up to 20 percent if the product does not sell as expected. This gives quite a bit of flexibility.

However, if the forecast is off by more than 20 percent, problems arise. If demand is greater than that limit, sales will be lost—perhaps to a competitor with better product availability. If demand is more than 20 percent lower than the production order quantity, there will be excess inventory of out-of-date software at the end of the year. To limit costs of this sort, excess inventory is transferred to an export agent for sale in a foreign market. This involves added costs—tariffs, agent fees, and shipping—and it isn't possible to recover the full unit production cost on these units. Therefore, if the firm overproduces in any year, the marketing department budget is charged. The charge is 15 percent of the production cost for all units shipped to overseas markets.

CONCLUSION

This memorandum overviews the major strategy decision areas that must be considered in developing the marketing plan. It also reviews issues that should be considered in making decisions in each of these areas.

One final point should be emphasized. Each year, after the marketing plan has been developed, it must be submitted to the president for final approval. So that the president can quickly overview the full set of decisions you've made, these decisions are to be submitted on a special summary form. Sometimes the president asks for other supporting documentation. The president will tell you what you need to do in that area. But it is very important to meet the deadline for submitting your plan. If you miss the deadline, it may not be possible to make desired product changes in time or to meet production schedules. Other serious problems may also arise. In fact, if the plan is late the president may have no alternative except to simply authorize a continuation of the plan you submitted in the previous period. Obviously, that wouldn't leave the president with a good impression of the people in the marketing department. Therefore, meeting the deadline is critical.

4
Submitting the Marketing Plan

Note: Depending on the scope of your responsibilities, you will be told to read this chapter or to read Chapter 5 instead. At this point, you don't need to read both.

The president requests that you submit a form summarizing your annual plan. The president instructed a staff assistants to provide you with a copy of the form and any related information you might need. In addition, the president asked the assistant to provide you with a copy of the firm's most recent financial summary and examples of other reports that are available annually. This chapter is the material prepared by the president's assistant.

MARKETING PLAN DECISION FORM

After you develop your annual marketing plan, the president wants you to submit a summary form that overviews your decisions.

The previous marketing manager already reviewed the strategy decision areas covered by the form *(see previous chapter)*. But—for your reference in completing the form—a concise summary of his major points is provided on the next page. There is also a copy of the Marketing Plan Decision Form (Exhibit 4A). In fact, this is the completed form submitted by the previous marketing manager at the beginning of this past year. It summarizes last year's decisions.

The form and notes are simple and clear—so they do not need further explanation here. The president will set the deadline for you to submit your decisions. The president will also tell you if you need to submit any other information along with the summary.

Guide to the Marketing Plan Decision Form (Level 1)

Number of Sales Reps:
The number of sales representatives must be specified for each channel. Each sales rep earns $20,000 per year in salary. Each sales rep that is fired receives $5,000 in severance pay.

Distribution Intensity:
The distribution intensity level (percent of dealers) must be specified for each channel. The minimum value is 0, implying no distribution in that channel. Otherwise, the percentage should be between the extremes of 1 percent (extremely exclusive distribution) and a maximum of 100 percent (indicating very intensive distribution).

Customer Service:
The dollar amount that you want to spend on customer service, which must be greater than or equal to zero.

Brand Name
The brand name may be up to 10 characters long. It is used for identification on reports, and thus should not be changed after it is set during the first period.

Brand Features
 Number of Special Commands:
The number of special commands must be between 5 and 20.

 Error Protection:
The error protection rating must be between 1 and 10. A higher rating corresponds to greater error protection.

 Ease of Learning:
This rating must be between 1 and 10. A higher rating corresponds to greater ease of learning.

Production Order Quantity:
The production order must be greater than or equal to 100. It should be within 20 percent of the demand for your brand to avoid inventory stockouts if you underproduce, or to avoid transfer charges resulting from excess inventory if you overproduce.

Advertising Dollars:
Advertising spending must be greater than or equal to zero.

Wholesale Price:
The wholesale price must be between $75 and $250. Your management will not accept a wholesale price below $75, and a wholesale price greater than $250 leads to retail prices higher than any consumers are willing to pay.

Marketing Research Reports:
You may purchase any of the following reports:
1. Market Share by Segment (all brands) — $15,000
2. Market Share by Channel (all brands) — $12,000
3. Consumer Preference Study — $30,000
4. Marketing Effectiveness Report — $25,000
5. Detailed Sales Analysis (own brand) — $15,000
6. Customer Shopping Habits — $7,000

Exhibit 4A

THE MARKETING GAME! Decision Form
Level 1

Industry [ ]   **Firm** [ ]   **Period** [ ]

	Channel 1	Channel 2
Number of Sales Reps :	10	10
Distribution Intensity :	30%	30%

Customer Service: $ 92,500

Brand Name: *Firm X*

Brand Features:

Number of Special Commands (5 - 20): 8

Error Protection (1 - 10): 3

Ease of Learning (1 -10) : 3

Production Order Quantity: 25,000

Advertising Dollars : $ 250,000

Wholesale Price : $ 95.00

	1	2	3	4	5	6
Marketing Research Reports (Y/N) :	Y	Y	N	Y	Y	N

Check here if exceptional items are noted on back of form: [ ]

Exhibit 4A (continued)

Exceptional Items:

Purchase of Additional Marketing Research: _____

Fines: _____

Budget Modifications: _____

Additional Information:

_____

_____

_____

_____

_____

_____

Signature of Firm's Representative: _____

Signature of Instructor: _____

Guide to Market Research Reports:

1. Market Share by Segment (all brands)
2. Market Share by Channel (all brands)
3. Consumer Preference Study
4. Marketing Effectiveness Report
5. Detailed Sales Analysis (own brand)
6. Customer Shopping Habits Study

FEEDBACK FOR CONTROL AND PLANNING

At the end of each year, you will receive important feedback about the performance of your plan. You'll get the following reports:
1. annual financial summary (including your budget for the next period),
2. a production summary,
3. the industry sales report,
4. the industry product features and prices report,
5. the industry marketing activity report, and
6. any additional marketing research reports you have purchased.

These reports should be used for control purposes—and as a basis for future planning. Exhibit 4B—which starts on page 47 and continues for four pages—provides copies of the latest set of reports (i.e., from the previous period).

Please study these reports before developing your plan. They show the results produced by the marketing plan decisions submitted last year by the previous marketing manager (see page 43). They also summarize the firm's current financial position, your budget for next period, and other important information.

ANNUAL FINANCIAL SUMMARY

The Financial Summary is clearly labeled and does not need much additional explanation. A few comments, however, may be helpful.

The unit cost, $47.00, is what it cost per unit to produce multimedia software with the features specified by the previous marketing manager.

Gross sales is the revenue received from sales to dealers. You can confirm that gross sales is equal to the units sold multiplied by the *wholesale* price charged to dealers.

The cost of goods sold is computed by multiplying the number of units sold by the unit cost. (Note: some accountants refer to cost of goods sold by some other name, such as cost of sales. This firm has been using the term cost of goods sold for some time, so that term has been retained for consistency).

The gross margin is the money left after cost of goods sold is subtracted from gross sales. The gross margin is used to cover other costs and contribute to profits.

The various expense items are the costs of the marketing plan submitted by the previous marketing manager. You may wish to cross-check these expenses against the Marketing Plan Decision Form he submitted.

Net contribution to profit (or loss) is what is left after subtracting expenses from the gross margin.

At the bottom of the financial summary is the budget that the president has set aside for the marketing department for next year. As you can see, you have up to $984,000 to spend. Based on trade association data, this amount represents about 25 percent of what all four firms in this industry will spend on marketing.

PRODUCTION SUMMARY

The Production Summary shows requested production—the production order quantity submitted by the previous marketing manager based on his forecast of demand. Actual production was slightly higher—to meet demand for the 25,151 units actually sold. There was no excess inventory at the end of the year, so there were no transfer charges for overseas sales.

MARKETING RESEARCH REPORTS

The various marketing research reports have already been described *(see Chapter 3)*. But Exhibit 4B provides the actual reports for this year.

Two of the marketing research reports in Exhibit 4B warrant comment. Specifically, the Customer Shopping Habits report has never been purchased by the firm, and as a result the information found in this report is not available to the firm. However, the sample shows the general format used in this report. If you buy this report from the marketing research firm in the future, you will get a completed report that shows the proportion of consumers from different segments who shop in each of the channels.

Similarly, the firm did not purchase the Consumer Preferences Report last year. However, the firm has purchased it in the past—and the tables shows a range of estimates based on past reports. However, if you buy this report from the marketing research firm in the future, you will get a current report that should be more precise (within the error due to survey sampling) with estimates of average consumer preferences for different features (by segment).

Exhibit 4B
Company Report for Previous Period

```
*************** Financial Summary ***************

FIRM X              Channel 1        Channel 2         Total
-------
Units Sold              14074            11077         25151
Wholesale Price        $95.00           $95.00
Unit Cost              $47.00           $47.00

Gross Sales        $1,337,030       $1,052,315    $2,389,345
Cost of Goods Sold   $661,478         $520,619    $1,182,097
Transfer Charges                                          $0
Gross Margin                                      $1,207,248

Expenses
Advertising                                         $250,000
Sales Force -Salary  $200,000         $200,000      $400,000
       -Firing Costs                                      $0
       -Commission    $66,852          $52,616      $119,468
Customer Service                                     $92,500
R&D for Product Modifications                             $0
Marketing Research                                   $67,000
Total Expenses                                      $928,968

Net Contribution (Loss)                             $278,280


    Budget for Next Period:   $984,000    ( 25% of Industry Total)
```

```
*************** Production Summary ***************

         Requested     Actual      Units      Inventory     Unit
Brand    Production    Production   Sold       Transferred   Cost
         _____      _____     ____       _____      ____

FIRM X    25000         25151       25151          0         $47.
```

Exhibit 4B (continued)

**************** Industry Sales Report ****************

Multimedia Software Brand	Unit Sales	Market Share (Units)	$ Sales	Market Share ($ Sales)
FIRM 1	25,151	0.250	$4,292,964	0.250
FIRM 2	25,151	0.250	$4,292,964	0.250
FIRM 3	25,151	0.250	$4,292,964	0.250
FIRM 4	25,151	0.250	$4,292,964	0.250
Total	100,604		$17,171,854	

Channel	Unit Sales	$ Sales
1	56,296	$10,696,240
2	44,308	$6,475,614

********** Product Features & Prices Report ***********

Multimedia Software Brand	Special Commands	Error Protection	Ease of Learning	Average Retail Price Channel 1	Average Retail Price Channel 2
FIRM 1	8	3	3	$190.00	$146.15
FIRM 2	8	3	3	$190.00	$146.15
FIRM 3	8	3	3	$190.00	$146.15
FIRM 4	8	3	3	$190.00	$146.15

*************** Marketing Activity Report ***************
(Data Reported Is for Period 0)

	FIRM 1	FIRM 2	FIRM 3	FIRM 4
Advertising Dollars	$250,000	$250,000	$250,000	$250,000
Advertising Type				
Sales Promotion				
-Channel 1	$0	$0	$0	$0
-Channel 2	$0	$0	$0	$0
Number of Sales Reps				
-Channel 1	10	10	10	10
-Channel 2	10	10	10	10
Commission Rate	5%	5%	5%	5%
Customer Service	$92,500	$92,500	$92,500	$92,500

Exhibit 4B (continued)

********** Report 1: Market Share By Segment ***********

Segment Brand	Students	Home	Assistants	Artists	Managers	Parents
FIRM 1	0.250	0.250	0.250	0.250	0.250	0.250
FIRM 2	0.250	0.250	0.250	0.250	0.250	0.250
FIRM 3	0.250	0.250	0.250	0.250	0.250	0.250
FIRM 4	0.250	0.250	0.250	0.250	0.250	0.250
Total Sales (in Units)	20,028	15,084	25,104	10,240	22,056	8,092

********** Report 2: Market Share By Channel **********

Brand	Channel 1	Channel 2
FIRM 1	0.250	0.250
FIRM 2	0.250	0.250
FIRM 3	0.250	0.250
FIRM 4	0.250	0.250
Total Sales (in Units)	56,296	44,308

******* Report 3: Average Customer Preferences[a] ********

Segment	Special Commands	Error Protection	Ease of Learning	Price Range
Students	10-13	2-4	1-3	low
Home	7-10	2-4	6-8	low
Assistants	10-13	6-8	6-8	high
Artists	12-15	2-4	4-6	high
Managers	13-16	6-8	2-4	high
Parents	5-8	2-4	7-3	low

[a]Note: the numbers in this table are simply estimates based on reports from previous periods; this report was not purchased in the current period.

Exhibit 4B (continued)

```
******* Report 4: Marketing Effectiveness Report ******

                                           # of              # of
                                       Competitors      Competitors with
                                       with Lower       Equal or Higher
                              Index       Index              Index
                              ------      ------             ------

Awareness - FIRM X            0.550         0                  3

Customer Service
   Consumer Group Rating       100%
   Industry Average Rating     100%

Channel 1:
   Sales Rep Workload Index     100%
   Dealer Satisfaction         1.000         0                  3
   Channel Strength ("Push")   0.500         0                  3

Channel 2
   Sales Rep Workload Index     100%
   Dealer Satisfaction         1.000         0                  3
   Channel Strength ("Push")    .500         0                  3




********** Report 5: Detailed Sales Analysis **********

Segment   Students    Home   Assistants Artists   Managers  Parents
          -------    -------  -------    -------    -------   -------

FIRM X
-Channel 1    708      936     5,080      1,578     4,752     1,020
-Channel 2  4,299    2,835     1,196        982       762     1,003




**********Report 6: Customer Shopping Habits **********

                       Percent          Percent
                      of Shopping      of Shopping
                          in               in
             Segment   Channel 1        Channel 2
             -------   ---------        ---------

             Students      ?                ?
             Home          ?                ?
             Assistants    ?                ?
             Artists       ?                ?
             Managers      ?                ?
             Parents       ?                ?
```

Note: this report has not previously been purchased, which explains why the proportion of consumers in each segment shopping in each channel is not reported; however, the proportions would be reported if the current report is purchased.

5
Submitting an Expanded Marketing Plan

Note: Depending on the scope of your responsibilities, you will be told to read Chapter 4 or to read this chapter instead. Unless you are instructed otherwise, you don't need to read both.

The president has decided to expand the responsibilities of the marketing department. In addition, the president wants you to submit a form summarizing your marketing plan. The president asked a staff assistant to prepare a memo to tell you what you need to do. The president also asked the assistant to provide you with a copy of the firm's most recent financial summary and examples of other reports that are available annually. This chapter is the material prepared by the president's assistant.

INTRODUCTION

Each year, the marketing manager submits a form summarizing key marketing plan decisions. The president has decided to ask for more detail on this form than has been requested in the past. In addition, the president has decided to expand marketing department responsibilities in several areas. This memo reviews these changes. In addition, a copy of the expanded Marketing Plan Decision Form (Level 2) is included. Finally, several reports that give you important information about the firm and the results of last year's marketing plan are discussed.

EXPANDED RESPONSIBILITIES

Price

The legal department has recommended to the president that the marketing department be allowed to set different wholesale prices for dealers in the two channels. The firm's lawyers have concluded that this will not result in legal problems.

Promotion

• Personal Selling

The president has decided that the marketing department should be allowed to set the sales force commission percent—which company policy previously set at 5 percent of sales. A higher commission rate might increase sales rep motivation—but, of course, it is a selling expense that is subtracted from gross margin in arriving at profit contribution. The president has requested that the commission rate not exceed 15 percent—so that sales compensation does not get totally out of line with other pay rates in the firm.

In the past, the president has had a policy that sales reps spend approximately 10 percent of their time on support (non-selling) activities. However, the president is not certain that the policy makes sense. So, it is now a marketing department responsibility to decide, for each channel, what percent of a sales rep's time should be spent on support activities. This gives you new flexibility to make more effective use of the the sales force. You can even specify that sales reps spend no time on support activities. However, the president has directed that at least half of sales force time be devoted to selling activities.

• Advertising

In the past, the marketing manager and the ad agency worked out the details of what advertising would be done. Only the dollar amount to be spent on advertising was reported to the president on the Marketing Plan Decision Form. So that the president will have a better idea of how the money is going to be spent, please include information about the type of advertising you plan to use to achieve your marketing objectives. To keep the planning form concise, the president has asked that you simply indicate which type of advertising you will be using: pioneering advertising, direct competitive advertising, indirect competitive advertising, reminder advertising, or corporate (institutional) advertising.

• Sales Promotion

In the past, the firm only used sales promotion targeted at dealers only irregularly. Often no one considered promotion when developing the marketing plan, and if promotion was used, it was paid for with special funds. To encourage more careful planning of sales promotion, the president has asked that your marketing plan indicate how much you will be spending on promotion in each channel. Note that spending for sales (trade) promotion will now be charged to the marketing department budget.

Marketing Research

The office of the president has just received a letter from the outside marketing research firm that sells us the Consumer Preference Study (marketing research report 3). The letter explained that the research firm has developed a new "product positioning" study that might enable you to get a better idea of how well our software—and the products offered by competitors—are meeting the needs of different customer segments.

Specifically, the letter explains that the study uses a computerized approach called perceptual mapping to determine how closely our brand (and competitors' brands) match with the ideal brand for customers in each of the different segments. The results of the research are provided in a simple table, where each row in the table is for one of the four competing products, and where each column is for one of the six key market segments. The entries in the table can be thought of as "distances" of each of the brands from each segment's ideal points. Thus, a high number suggests a greater distance—and a brand that is not very similar to the segment's ideal. Conversely, a low number indicates a small distance, suggesting that a brand is quite similar to the segment's ideal. The marketing research firm says that it will not reveal the details of the propriety procedure it uses to develop these summary measures. However, a well known marketing professor from a major business school has certified that the firm is using a "state of the art" method that should be very accurate.

The marketing research firm has priced the report at $30,000. While the report is expensive, the president has authorized the marketing department to pay for the report from its budget if it appears that the expense is justified. If you would like to include a purchase of this new report in your marketing plan, it appears on the Marketing Plan Decision Form (Level 2) as marketing research report 7.

MARKETING PLAN DECISION FORM

Exhibit 5A (starting on page 55) is a copy of the firm's Expanded Marketing Plan Decision Form (Level 2). A concise set of instructions for completing the form begins on page 54. The blanks on the form have been filled in with the most recent decisions made by the previous marketing manager—so the form also summarizes last year's marketing plan. In the past, the marketing manager did not need to indicate the type of advertising that would be used—so that part of the form has been left blank. The form and notes are simple and clear—so they do not need further explanation here. The president will tell you the deadline by which you will need to submit your decisions. You will also be informed if you are expected to submit any other information along with the summary.

Guide to the Marketing Plan Decision Form (Level 2):

Number of Sales Reps: The number of sales representatives must be specified for each channel. Each sales rep earns $20,000 per year in salary. Each sales rep that is fired receives $5,000 in severance pay.

Distribution Intensity: The distribution intensity level (percent of dealers) must be specified for each channel. The minimum value is 0, implying no distribution in that channel. Otherwise, the percentage should be between the extremes of 1 percent (extremely exclusive distribution) and a maximum of 100 percent (indicating very intensive distribution).

Percent Non-Selling Time: This determines how much time each sales representative spends on support activities. The range is from 0 percent to 50 percent.

Sales Commission: The minimum commission rate is 5 percent, and the maximum is 15 percent.

Customer Service: The dollar amount that you spend on customer service must be greater than or equal to zero.

Brand name: The brand name may be up to 10 characters long. It is used for identification on reports, and thus should not be changed once it is set in the first period..

Brand Features
Number of Special Commands: The number of special commands must be between 5 and 20.
Error Protection: The error protection rating must be between 1 and 10. A higher rating corresponds to greater error protection.
Ease of Learning This rating must be between 1 and 10. A higher rating corresponds to greater ease of learning.

Production Order Quantity: The production order must be greater than or equal to 100. It should be within 20 percent of the demand for your brand to avoid inventory stockouts if you underproduce, or to avoid transfer charges resulting from excess inventory if you overproduce.

Advertising Dollars: Advertising spending must be greater than or equal to zero.

Type of advertising: P = pioneering; D = direct competitive; I = indirect competitive; R = reminder; C = corporate (institutional)

Wholesale Price: The wholesale price must be between $75 and $250; set a price for each channel. Your management will not accept a wholesale price below $75, and a wholesale price greater than $250 leads to retail prices higher than any consumers are willing to pay.

Marketing Research Reports: You may purchase any of the following reports:
1. Market Share by Segment (all brands) — $15,000
2. Market Share by Channel (all brands) — $12,000
3. Consumer Preference Study — $30,000
4. Marketing Effectiveness Report — $25,000
5. Detailed Sales Analysis (own brand) — $15,000
6. Customer Shopping Habits — $7,000
7. Product positioning Report — $30,000

Exhibit 5A

THE MARKETING GAME! Decision Form
Level 2

Industry [ ] **Firm** [ ] **Period** [ ]

	Channel 1	Channel 2
Number of Sales Reps :	10	10
Distribution Intensity:	30%	30%
Percent Non-Selling Time (0 - 50) :	10%	10%

Sales Commission (0 - 15) : 5 %

Customer Service: $ 92,500

Brand Name: FIRM X

Brand Features:

Number of Special Commands (5 - 20): 8

Error Protection (1 - 10): 3

Ease of Learning (1 -10) : 3

Production Order Quantity: 25,000

Advertising Dollars : $ 250,000

Type of Advertising : [ ]
(P,D,I,R,C)

	Channel 1	Channel 2
Wholesale Prices :	$ 95.00	$ 95.00
Sales Promotion:	$ 0	$ 0

Marketing Research Reports (Y/N) :	1	2	3	4	5	6	7
	Y	Y	N	Y	Y	N	N

Check here if exceptional items are noted on back of form: [ ]

Exhibit 5A (continued)

Exceptional Items:

Purchase of Additional Marketing Research: _____

Fines: _____

Budget Modifications: _____

Additional Information:

_____

_____

_____

_____

_____

_____

Signature of Firm's Representative: _____

Signature of Instructor: _____

Guide to Market Research Reports:
1. Market Share by Segment (all brands)
2. Market Share by Channel (all brands)
3. Consumer Preference Study
4. Marketing Effectiveness Report
5. Sales by Segment by Channel (own brand)
6. Consumer Shopping Habits Study
7. Product Positioning Report

Guide to Advertising Types:
P: Pioneering
D: Direct Competitive
I: Indirect Competitive
R: Reminder
C: Corporate or Institutional

FEEDBACK FOR CONTROL AND PLANNING

At the end of each year, you will receive important feedback about your plan's performance. You'll get the following reports:
1. annual financial summary,
2. a production summary,
3. the industry sales report,
4. the industry product features and prices report,
5. the industry marketing activity report, and
6. any additional marketing research reports you have purchased.

These reports should be used for control purposes—and as a basis for future planning. The format of some of these reports has just recently been modified to provide the marketing department with more detailed feedback—reflecting the expanded decision areas. However, the information from the latest set of reports has been organized into the new format—so you will know what to expect. (See Exhibit 5B, starting on page 59.)

Please study these reports before developing your plan. They show the results produced by the marketing plan decisions submitted last year by the previous marketing manager. They also summarize the firm's current financial position, your budget for next period, and other important information.

ANNUAL FINANCIAL SUMMARY

The Financial Summary is clearly labeled and does not need much additional explanation. A few comments, however, may be helpful to you.

The unit cost, $47.00, is what it cost per unit to produce multimedia software with the features specified by the previous marketing manager.

Gross sales is the revenue received from sales to dealers. You can confirm that gross sales is equal to the units sold multiplied by the *wholesale* price.

The cost of goods sold is computed by multiplying the number of units sold by the unit cost. (Note: some accountants refer to cost of goods sold by some other name, such as cost of sales. This firm has been using the term cost of goods sold for some time, so that term has been retained for consistency).

The gross margin is the money left after cost of goods sold is subtracted from gross sales.

The various expense items are the costs of the marketing plan submitted by the previous marketing manager. You may wish to cross-check this against the Marketing Plan Decision Form he submitted.

Net contribution to profit (or loss) is what is left after subtracting expenses from the gross margin.

At the bottom of the financial summary is the budget that the president has set aside for the marketing department for next year. As you can see, you have up to $984,000 to spend. Based on trade association data, this amount represents about 25 percent of what all four firms in this industry will spend on marketing.

PRODUCTION SUMMARY

The Production Summary shows requested production—the production order quantity submitted by the previous marketing manager based on his forecast of demand. Actual production was slightly higher—to meet demand for the 25,151 units actually sold. There was no excess inventory at the end of the year, so there were no transfer charges for overseas sales.

MARKETING RESEARCH REPORTS

The various marketing research reports have already been described *(see Chapter 3)*. But Exhibit 5B provides the actual reports for this year.

Three of the marketing research reports in Exhibit 5B warrant comment. Specifically, the Customer Shopping Habits report has never been purchased by the firm, and as a result the information found in this report is not available. However, the sample table shows the general format used in this report. If you buy this report from the marketing research firm in the future, you will get a completed report that shows the proportion of consumers from different segments who shop in each of the channels.

Similarly, the firm did not purchase the Consumer Preferences Report last year. However, the firm has purchased it in the past—and the tables shows a range of estimates based on past reports. However, if you buy this report from the marketing research firm in the future, you will get a current report that should be more precise (within the error due to survey sampling) with estimates of average consumer preferences for different features (by segment).

Finally, as noted earlier, marketing research report 7 has not previously been available from the marketing research firm. However, the sample in Exhibit 5B shows its general format—based on the marketing research firm's description.

Exhibit 5B
Company Report for Previous Period

```
*************** Financial Summary ***************

FIRM X                  Channel 1        Channel 2         Total
-------
Units Sold                  14074            11077          25151
Wholesale Price            $95.00           $95.00
Unit Cost                  $47.00           $47.00

Gross Sales            $1,337,030       $1,052,315     $2,389,345
Cost of Goods Sold       $661,478         $520,619     $1,182,097
Transfer Charges                                               $0
Gross Margin                                           $1,207,248

Expenses
Advertising                                              $250,000
Sales Force -Salary      $200,000         $200,000       $400,000
            -Firing Costs                                      $0
            -Commission    $66,852          $52,616       $119,468
Customer Service                                          $92,500
Sales Promotion                $0               $0             $0
R&D for Product Modifications                                  $0
Marketing Research                                       $67,000
Total Expenses                                           $928,968

Net Contribution (Loss)                                 $278,280


   Budget for Next Period:   $984,000    ( 25% of Industry Total)
```

```
*************** Production Summary ***************

          Requested      Actual       Units      Inventory      Unit
Brand     Production    Production     Sold      Transferred     Cost
-----     ----------    ----------    -----      -----------    ----

FIRM X      25000         25151        25151          0         $47.
```

Exhibit 5B (continued)

*************** Industry Sales Report ***************

Multimedia Software Brand	Unit Sales	Market Share (Units)	$ Sales	Market Share ($ Sales)
FIRM 1	25,151	0.250	$4,292,964	0.250
FIRM 2	25,151	0.250	$4,292,964	0.250
FIRM 3	25,151	0.250	$4,292,964	0.250
FIRM 4	25,151	0.250	$4,292,964	0.250
Total	100,604		$17,171,854	

Channel	Unit Sales	$ Sales
1	56,296	$10,696,240
2	44,308	$6,475,614

********** Product Features & Prices Report ***********

Multimedia Software Brand	Special Commands	Error Protection	Ease of Learning	Average Retail Price Channel 1	Average Retail Price Channel 2
FIRM 1	8	3	3	$190.00	$146.15
FIRM 2	8	3	3	$190.00	$146.15
FIRM 3	8	3	3	$190.00	$146.15
FIRM 4	8	3	3	$190.00	$146.15

*************** Marketing Activity Report ***************
(Data Reported Is for Period 0)

	FIRM 1	FIRM 2	FIRM 3	FIRM 4
Advertising Dollars	$250,000	$250,000	$250,000	$250,000
Advertising Type				
Sales Promotion				
-Channel 1	$0	$0	$0	$0
-Channel 2	$0	$0	$0	$0
Number of Sales Reps				
-Channel 1	10	10	10	10
-Channel 2	10	10	10	10
Commission Rate	5%	5%	5%	5%
Customer Service	$92,500	$92,500	$92,500	$92,500

Exhibit 5B (continued)

********** Report 1: Market Share By Segment ***********

Segment Brand	Students	Home	Assistants	Artists	Managers	Parents
FIRM 1	0.250	0.250	0.250	0.250	0.250	0.250
FIRM 2	0.250	0.250	0.250	0.250	0.250	0.250
FIRM 3	0.250	0.250	0.250	0.250	0.250	0.250
FIRM 4	0.250	0.250	0.250	0.250	0.250	0.250
Total Sales (in Units)	20,028	15,084	25,104	10,240	22,056	8,092

********** Report 2: Market Share By Channel **********

Brand	Channel 1	Channel 2
FIRM 1	0.250	0.250
FIRM 2	0.250	0.250
FIRM 3	0.250	0.250
FIRM 4	0.250	0.250
Total Sales (in Units)	56,296	44,308

******* Report 3: Average Customer Preferences ********

Segment	Special Commands	Error Protection	Ease of Learning	Price Range
Students	10-13	2-4	1-3	low
Home	7-10	2-4	6-8	low
Assistants	10-13	6-8	6-8	high
Artists	12-15	2-4	4-6	high
Managers	13-16	6-8	2-4	high
Parents	5-8	2-4	7-3	low

Exhibit 5B (continued)

```
******* Report 4: Marketing Effectiveness Report ******
```

	Index	# of Competitors with Lower Index	# of Competitors with Equal or Higher Index
	------	------	------
Awareness - FIRM X	0.550	0	3
Customer Service			
Consumer Group Rating	100%		
Industry Average Rating	100%		
Channel 1:			
Sales Rep Workload Index	100%		
Dealer Satisfaction	1.000	0	3
Channel Strength ("Push")	0.500	0	3
Channel 2			
Sales Rep Workload Index	100%		
Dealer Satisfaction	1.000	0	3
Channel Strength ("Push")	.500	0	3

```
********** Report 5: Detailed Sales Analysis **********
```

Segment	Students	Home	Assistants	Artists	Managers	Parents
	-------	-------	-------	-------	-------	-------
FIRM X						
-Channel 1	708	936	5,080	1,578	4,752	1,020
-Channel 2	4,299	2,835	1,196	982	762	1,003

```
**********Report 6: Customer Shopping Habits **********
```

Segment	Percent of Shopping in Channel 1	Percent of Shopping in Channel 2
-------	---------	---------
Students	?	?
Home	?	?
Assistants	?	?
Artists	?	?
Managers	?	?
Parents	?	?

Exhibit 5B (continued)

```
******** Report 7: Product Positioning Report *********

Brand     Students    Home    Assistants Artists   Managers   Parents
------    -------    -------    -------    -------    -------    -------

Firm1        ?          ?          ?          ?          ?          ?
Firm2        ?          ?          ?          ?          ?          ?
Firm3        ?          ?          ?          ?          ?          ?
Firm4        ?          ?          ?          ?          ?          ?
```

6
Supporting the Marketing Plan

Note: A staff assistant in the president's office was instructed to provide you with copies of several standard forms that have been routinely used in the company and to briefly explain the purpose of the forms. This is the set of notes prepared by the president's staff assistant.

From time to time, the president may ask you to submit a special report about your marketing strategy or other details of the marketing plan. The president will let you know if and when there is a special request. The president may also ask you to provide supporting information along with the annual Marketing Plan Decision Form. For example, you may be asked to submit an analysis of how much profit you expect to make based on the marketing plan. To make it easier to prepare this analysis, use the Marketing Budget Planning Form.[1] A concise set of directions for completing the form appears on the next page opposite a copy of the form (Exhibit 6A). Even if the president does not ask you to submit this information, you can use the form to evaluate the likely profitability of your plan and to compare it against the actual results you receive later in the Annual Financial Summary.

On the back of the Marketing Budget Planning Form is a Marketing Strategy Summary Form (Exhibit 6B). You can use this form to briefly describe your planned marketing strategy and discuss the nature of competition the firm can expect to face. Again, the president may ask you to complete and submit this form. Either way, summarizing your ideas on the form can help you to keep an organized record of your strategy. It can be very helpful to have a written record of your strategy and how it changes over time.

---

[1]You may also use the PLAN software, described in Appendix A after Chapter 7, to prepare a financial analysis (pro forma) of the results you expect from a plan.

Chapter 6

Guide to Budget Planning Form

1. Estimated Unit Sales: Enter the *expected* unit sales for each channel and the total.

2. Wholesale Price: Enter your wholesale price for each channel.

3. Unit Cost: Compute unit cost as follows:

    $4 × (Number of Special Commands)
    + $3 × (Error Protection Rating)
    + $2 × (Ease of Learning Rating).

4. Gross Sales: For each channel, multiply *unit sales* by *wholesale price* to determine gross sales. Add channel gross sales to get total.

5. Cost of Goods Sold: For each channel, multiply *unit sales* by *unit cost* to determine cost of goods sold. Add channel cost of goods sold to get total.

6. Gross Margin: Subtract *total cost of goods sold* from *total gross sales* to determine the gross margin.

7. Advertising: Enter your advertising expenses for the period.

8. Sales Force - Salary: Compute salary expense for each channel by multiplying the number of sales representatives by $20,000.

9. Sales Force - Firing Cost: If the total number of sales representatives is less than last period's total, you must pay each fired sales representative $5,000 in severance pay.

10. Sales Force - Commission: Compute commission expense for each channel by multiplying *unit sales* by *wholesale price* times *commission rate*.

11. Customer Service: Enter your customer service expense for the period

12. Sales Promotion: (optional) Enter your sales promotion expense for each channel.

13. R&D for Product Modifications: If you have changed the features of your product, enter total product modifications expense for the period. (see page 30.)

14. Market Research: Enter total cost of market research reports for the period. Costs for the reports are:

    Report 1: $15,000   Report 2: $12,000
    Report 3: $30,000   Report 4: $25,000
    Report 5: $15,000   Report 6: $ 7,000
    Report 7: $30,000 (optional, level 2 only)

15. Total Expenses: Add expenses (Advertising through market research) to determine total expenses for the period.

16. Net Contribution: Compute net profit contribution by subtracting *total expenses* from the *gross margin*.

17. Spending Against Budget Subtract *Sales Force Commission expense* from *Total Expenses (on line 15)*

7
A New Market Opportunity

Note: In an earlier report to the president of your firm, Market-Views, Inc.—a consulting firm—casually recommended that the firm consider adding another product. The president asked that Market-Views elaborate on the basis for that recommendation in a brief report. This is the text of Market-Views' report.

PURPOSE

Your firm currently develops and markets multimedia software for microcomputers. Yet it would be short-sighted to define your market just in terms of the product you offer. Customers in the broad product-market in which you now compete have needs that are not being met by existing products. There is a possible opportunity for the firm to meet these needs and improve profits. The new opportunity might involve another target market and marketing mix in addition to the firm's current strategy. The opportunity could also take advantage of a number of the firm's strengths and resources.

The purpose of this report is to discuss this potential opportunity. First, several relevant trends in the external environment are reviewed. Next, a new product opportunity relevant to those trends is described. Then, the needs of homogeneous sub-markets within the broad product-market are described. The report concludes with a brief discussion of some of the ways that product, place, promotion, and price decisions would need to be blended to develop an effective overall marketing program.

TRENDS IN THE EXTERNAL ENVIRONMENT

When personal computers first became popular, most people were only interested in running one basic application—like wordprocessing or a spreadsheet—at a time. However, as microcomputer users became more accustomed to the benefits of microcomputers and microcomputer software, they started using them in more and different ways. For example, some people kept a complete schedule of all their appointments on the computer. Some use the computer for financial calculations. Others use the computer to take notes while talking on the telephone—or to display a reminder message when it is time to go to a meeting. Other more specialized uses also exist, and in most cases specially designed programs make it easy to handle the jobs that need to be done.

In the past, programs for these special-purpose applications could not be used at the same time as some other software application—like wordprocessing. For example, if a manager was preparing a draft of a report on the wordprocessor and needed to do some calculations to be included in the report, it was necessary to leave the wordprocessing software, do the calculations with a different program, and then go back and start over with the wordprocessing software. It could be done—but it wasn't very convenient.

Desktop Software Set the Stage

To make quick switching between tasks (and different software programs) even more convenient, companies like Microsoft and IBM offered operating systems such as Windows and OS/2 that included a small set of "desktop" software. Desktop software handled a variety of needs that in the past might have been handled by a collection of different desktop items—like calculators, telephones, note pads, telephone directories, calendars, alarm clocks, and appointment books. Moreover, the desktop software was always ready to be used—even in the middle of some other job. Users could temporarily interrupt one job while they completed a special desktop application, and then instantly switch back again to the exact point where they left off.

Multimedia Personal Information Management (P.I.M.) Software—A New Concept

Standard desktop software has become popular among users of most types of computers. In fact, computer industry experts are now seeing the great potential for multimedia-enhanced versions of such desktop software. They refer to this product concept as multimedia *Personal Information Management* software—or P.I.M. software for short. Some firms developed and offered P.I.M software for early multimedia computers that used the Windows operating system, but most of these introductory efforts were not very successful. The technical problems with the computer hardware were too great a limitation.

No P.I.M. software is yet available for the special computer that uses your multimedia software. In fact, most firms cannot get the necessary technical details about this computer's propriety multimedia interfaces to develop such software. However, this computer should be the ideal "platform" for development of the multimedia P.I.M. market. Moreover, because of your license relationship with the computer producer, you can get the needed technical information.

Of course, the three other firms that have a similar relationship with the producer can also get this information—so there might be some competition. And the license agreement with the computer producer sets out a communications standard that must be followed by your firm or any of the others in your industry; thus, P.I.M. software that works on this machine will work with any other software a user already has (such as standard multimedia software)—even if that software was produced by another firm.

A few examples will help to give you an idea of what P.I.M. software can do—and how it is different from standard desktop software. For example, in the middle of preparing a report or presentation with a multimedia program, an administrative assistant might stop to answer a phone call from the boss with a request to set up a meeting. With the press of a key on the computer or with a spoken command, the assistant can instantly activate a special calendar program used to schedule appointments. Then, after the assistant prepares a list of names of the people who need to be at the meeting, the multimedia computer can be instructed to call the voice mail number (through the computer's telephone interface) for each person and leave whatever oral message the assistant has recorded. The multimedia computer and P.I.M. software handles this "in the background"—while the assistant returns to work on the presentation.

Similarly, with P.I.M software users can keep a complete schedule of all their appointments on the computer, along with a recorded voice message reminder concerning any details of the appointment; then they set a "timer" that plays the reminder message over the computer's speakers at the appropriate time. Other people might use the computer's telephone interface to serve as a voice mail (answering machine) system. Some other potential applications are simpler—like being able to quickly find and display a certain picture or video clip on the computer's screen. Many other specialized uses exist. Some—but not all—of these needs can be met with standard multimedia software. However, specially designed P.I.M. software would handle these jobs more easily and quickly.

Even with a few other firms a potential competitors in the same broad product-market for P.I.M. software, it may be possible to avoid head-to-head competition by identifying a homogeneous target market (based on one or more sub-markets) and targeting those customers with a specially blended marketing mix. Some of the possible segmentation and target marketing opportunities are reviewed next.

PRODUCT-MARKET SEGMENTS

The broad product-market in this area is quite heterogeneous. Different people have different reasons for wanting P.I.M. software, and they use it in different ways. But there are more homogeneous market segments within the broad product-market.

In fact, the people who are aggregated into distinct segments with respect to multimedia software needs also tend to share common preferences for P.I.M. software. The general characteristics of these segments have been described in an earlier report. Here, the focus is on the benefits they seek from P.I.M. software.

The Modern Students

Students often have to go to a microcomputer center on campus to do their computer work. As a result, they have less need for P.I.M. software than a person who is using a microcomputer at his or her own desk. In addition, many students think that P.I.M. software is less essential for their school work than multimedia software. On the other hand, some students do want the convenience of a few basic P.I.M. applications. For example, business students like to be able to "pop up" a graphics program while using multimedia software to work on a presentation or project assignment. Since students do not use the software frequently, they want it to be easy so they can remember how to use the programs that perform different tasks.

The Home Producers

Many of the people in this segment really like the idea of P.I.M. software. One important reason is that more than one person in the family typically uses the computer. P.I.M. software makes it possible for one person to be using the computer—and still let another family member interrupt briefly to do a quick job on a P.I.M. program. In addition, different members of the family may use different P.I.M. capabilities for different tasks. A busy Little League coach, for example, may use the computer to call kids on the team with a computer generated "message" about a change in practice time. Someone else may want to quickly check a segment of a cooking school full motion video "tutorial" for the ingredients needed for the evening meal. Someone else must just want to quickly select a photograph from a multimedia archive and include it in a computer generated birthday card. The home producers like the flexibility of P.I.M. software that can perform a number of different special-purpose tasks. But not everyone bothers to learn all of the possibilities. Rather, each person focuses on what they need most often. In short, people in this segment see P.I.M. software as a good way to get more use out of the computer. Moderately priced P.I.M. software makes it easier for family members to share the computer—and gives them added flexibility.

The Harried Assistants

The harried administrative assistants often must answer the phone, schedule appointments, and cope with other office jobs while doing wordprocessing or multimedia presentation work. Thus, good P.I.M. software can be quite useful to them. But, many firms have found that these employees feel overwhelmed when they have to learn more and more software to do every possible job on the computer. Company computer specialists can help set up the P.I.M. software for specific needs, and they can help train the administrative assistants. But that isn't enough. The trick is to achieve a balance between getting the most useful combination of P.I.M. tasks—and making certain that they are easy to use. If this balance can be achieved, the software pays for itself quickly. It helps the assistant save time, be better organized, and get more work done better.

The Commercial Artists

These people were often innovators in using multimedia software, and their response to P.I.M. software has been even more enthusiastic. They can dedicate the computer to their basic creative work—and still do a wide variety of quick jobs with P.I.M. programs as the need arises. In fact, they seem to be interested in P.I.M. software that can perform the widest array of tasks. They use the software a lot and don't seem to be put off by the technical details of learning what command is required to do what job. Perhaps this just reflects their confidence in using the computer. In addition, they see that the software saves them time for work. For them, software that saves time is a good business investment.

The High-Tech Managers

The high-tech managers like the idea of P.I.M. software, but it is less useful for them than for some other people. They are often out of the office and away from the computer. Someone else usually answers the phone for them—and takes messages or schedules appointments. Thus, managers who buy this software don't use it that often—and when they do use it, they are interested in a limited set of possible applications. Even though the company pays for the software, these managers realize that it would look foolish to spend a lot of money for a program that is not very critical to what they do. As a result, they are not willing to buy a very expensive program.

The Concerned Parents

Most members of this segment are not really in the market. They want their kids to have a good computer experience. Multimedia software helps to accomplish that objective. But P.I.M. software really isn't meant for kids. The few parents who express interest in this type of software seem to want a very simple program—one that just introduces the child to the idea. In general, they think that money is better spent in other ways.

MARKET POTENTIAL

The broad product-market for P.I.M. software appears to be late in the introductory part of the the product life cycle. Experts predict that the overall demand for P.I.M. software will not be as large as the demand for multimedia software—with the initial P.I.M. sales potential perhaps only about half what it is for multimedia software. But demand is expected to continue to grow for a number of years. In combination, this suggests that there should be profitable opportunities now and in the future.

The market potential for P.I.M. software is likely to depend on the same factors as the market potential for multimedia software. Specifically, these factors include the size of the different segments, growth trends, how well the marketing mix meets customers' needs, and the extent to which potential customers are aware of P.I.M. software and what it can do for them.

Your firm's previous experience with the segments in this market should give you some initial ideas about how the segments use software and about their consumer behavior. However, keep in mind that the growth trends for a new and different product may be quite different. Further, the target market that appears to offer your firm the best opportunities with multimedia software may not be the best target market for P.I.M. software.

Industry experts agree that the overall level of industry advertising will affect market growth. Many customers are still unfamiliar with P.I.M. software. Familiarity (and demand) are likely to increase if your firm—and competitors—spend money on advertising that helps to inform customers about the product class. But the product life cycle for this product is likely to move quite rapidly. Thus, it is hard to predict how quickly spending on pioneering advertising will be abandoned to support advertising with a competitive thrust. The transition may be very fast—especially if a number of competitors enter the market quickly.

As always, growth in the broad product-market—or in segments of the market—will depend on how well available marketing mixes meet customers' needs. Some customers may be willing to buy P.I.M. software that is not exactly what they want. They will probably just buy whatever comes closest to their ideal. On the other hand, many customers will continue to wait—and not buy anything until the right product is available in the right place at the right price. Further, different segments have different needs. Thus, different marketing strategies—different marketing mixes for different target markets—may be required.

This last point is an important one—so it is useful to consider several strategy decision areas within the 4Ps.

DEVELOPING THE MARKETING MIX

Product

There can be many technical differences in P.I.M. software. But research shows that most customers tend to simplify their evaluation process by grouping features into three main areas: (1) the number and variety of tasks (specialized applications within a P.I.M. program) available at the same time, (2) how similar the commands are for different applications, and (3) the extent to which the software can be customized by the user. Different customers seem to have quite different needs and interests with respect to these features, so it is useful to discuss them in more detail.

• Number of Tasks

All P.I.M. software support one or two basic tasks—like controlling a telephone dialer and message system or an alarm clock that allows the users to record special reminder messages. But it is possible to combine up to 9 or 10 different tasks within a single set of P.I.M. software. For example, it is possible to build P.I.M. programs that allow the user to play music CDs on the computer—while doing other work—or to search a multimedia database of pictures to quickly find a certain image. There are many other possibilities.

While it can be convenient to have the capability to handle a number of different tasks at the same time, not all customers want or need the variety. For example, it doesn't help to have software that will automatically dial a list of telephone numbers if the user's computer isn't hooked to the telephone—or if there are never more than a few numbers to dial. In addition, capability for P.I.M. software to handle a larger number of tasks requires much more computer memory, but not all customers' computers are equipped with extra memory.

There is another drawback. The likelihood of a problem or unintended side effect increases with the number of programs in operation at the same time. For example, a program that plays music CDs might work fine within a multimedia session. But if an alarm program rings a bell and tries to play a message over the computer's speakers at the same time the CD is playing, problems may occur. In some cases, the computer might even "lock up"—in which case the user's basic multimedia work may be lost. Computer magazines and software dealers will probably warn novice users to avoid such hassles—and stick to the basic combinations. Even so, some confident computer users love the flexibility of being able to handle as many P.I.M. tasks as possible.

• Similarity of Commands

Since particular applications for different tasks within P.I.M. software do quite specific things, they each contain only a few commands that are easy to learn. But there's a potential drawback here too. Since each application must have its own set of commands, the software may be designed so that the same commands are used in different applications—or each application may have its own unique commands. What's good is not always clear. It depends on the preferences of the user.

Having very similar commands across different programs makes them easier to use. But keeping everything consistent can be awkward when the tasks are different. For example, a certain key (command) might be used to set the time in an alarm clock program. The designer might try to use that same command in a similar way in a telephone dialing application. This sounds good, but what is the equivalent of setting the time in a dialing application? Is it selecting the telephone number, or is it setting the number of times to recall the number if it is busy the first time? Therefore, having similar commands for slightly different tasks may make operation more difficult. More experienced people who use P.I.M. software a lot become accustomed to the commands quickly—so they prefer that commands be different for different tasks. People who use P.I.M. software less frequently prefer that the commands be similar across programs.

• **Ability to Customize**

P.I.M. software is designed to function at the same time that another primary program (like multimedia or wordprocessing) is being used. But, this can create a problem. Sometimes there is a conflict between the P.I.M. software and the primary program. For example, a key combination or verbal command that is intended to delete a picture in a multimedia program may also be the key combination that causes a P.I.M. program—like an alarm clock—to pop up. After all, there are only so many combinations of commands that make sense. This problem can be avoided by allowing the user to install the P.I.M. programs with a personalized (custom) setup—making it faster to use both the primary program and the P.I.M. software.

But this customizing requires that the customer do more work initially and understand more technical details. It can take quite a bit of time—and it's easy to make errors. The software producer can provide detailed instructions that help to prevent problems—but the customer must still wade through all the technical detail and spend the time to get everything right.

Of course, customizing flexibility is not an all-or-nothing feature. Most software can be customized to some extent when it is installed. The real question is how much of this capability to build into the software. For example, at a simple level the customizing might allow a user to just indicate if the computer's stereo speakers can be used. At a more advanced level, the user might be able to customize 9 or 10 features. Adding more customizing adds to the cost of developing the software—but cost is not the only issue here. Some users will pay more if they can customize the P.I.M. programs to work well with other software they use. In short, the decision must be based on the needs and preferences of the specific target market at which the firm is aiming.

• **Product Modifications**

P.I.M. software is very dependent on the computer hardware. Thus, future changes in the computers will require that P.I.M. software be modified and updated. In addition, consumers' preferences for different types of P.I.M. software may change. This means that the software may need to be updated regularly. The annual computer trade show forces a schedule on this work. New software products must be ready in time for demonstrations at the trade show. Software dealers don't want to tie up money in software that they haven't actually tried at the trade show. Thus, if you introduce P.I.M. software, you will probably want to do it at the same time you release a modified version of your multimedia program.

Keep in mind that this could prove to be a very competitive market. If other firms are developing such software, they are keeping it a secret. Similarly, it would be wise for you to wait and announce your plans to the industry only after it is too late for a competitor to adjust for your actions.

• Product Costs

Based on data from your firm's accounting and R&D departments, it's possible to estimate several key costs relevant to the new product. These should be considered in any decision to introduce the new product and—if the product is introduced—in the annual marketing plan.

The initial cost to develop the new product—and the cost of any subsequent modifications—depends on the levels selected for the three product features. You can use the same approach to estimate initial development costs of the software and subsequent product modifications costs. The approach is summarized below:

P.I.M. Software R&D Product Modification Costs

FEATURE	FEASIBLE RANGE	Cost to Change Level from Previous Period	
		To Decrease Level	To Increase Level
Number of tasks	1-10	no cost	$8,000 × (change) × (change)
Similarity of commands	1-10	no cost	$5,000 × (change) × (change)
Ability to customize	1-10	$3,000 × (change)	$3,000 × (change) × (change)

In this table, change refers to the difference in the level of the feature from one period to the next. *The very first time the product is offered, the level of the feature is the amount of change—since the features would in effect start at the level 0.* Total product modification (or product development) cost is the sum of the costs to change individual features.

The level of the different product features will also directly affect the unit production cost. Specifically,

Unit production cost = $4 × (Number of tasks) +
$3 × (Similarity of commands) +
$2 × (Ability to customize).

Thus, the unit cost for P.I.M. software might vary from $9 to $90 depending on the features of the product.

Place

The new software could be distributed to the target market through the firm's existing channels of distribution. However, you may need to rethink your Place strategy. Experience in the multimedia software area indicates that different segments tend to prefer different channels. If the target market for your new marketing mix shops in a channel that you haven't emphasized in the past, you may need to recruit more or different middlemen.

On the other hand, it makes sense to blend your different strategies so that you take advantage of the channel relationships you have or can develop. Specifically, you may weaken your competitive position if you go after a target market best reached with a channel in which you have no strong market presence.

Further, you need to keep in mind that your channel focus will affect promotion decisions as well.

Promotion

Basically, you will face the same opportunities and limitations in promoting both P.I.M. and multimedia software. Thus, we will review issues in this area only briefly.

• Personal Selling

Having a second product could result in some economies of scale in personal selling. Sales reps spend much time traveling, planning, and doing other non-selling-related activities. But, once a rep is with the customer, it would not take long to discuss a second product. Of course, each rep could not cover as many accounts if there were more work to do at each account. But it is clear that a second product would not require doubling the size of the sales force.

How much additional selling effort might be required would depend on how selling effort is currently allocated between the two channels. If your new target market requires increased distribution intensity in one channel or the other, you may need to add quite a few sales reps. In addition, the type of channel that a rep calls on will influence how effort is split between selling and supporting activities.

Making these decisions wisely for two products—not just one—will be a bit more challenging. But the challenge is not so great that the opportunity should be screened out on this basis alone.

• Advertising

Advertising is another area where there might be efficiency in having two products. Your firm could advertise more that one product in an ad—and customer familiarity with one of your brands will probably have a positive spillover effect on the other. Of course, no advertising decision is ever simple. The advertising objectives for the new marketing mix or target market may be different than at present. And, advertising adjustments may be needed if the nature of competition is different for the two different products.

• Sales Promotion

Sales promotion can be used in basically the same way for P.I.M. software and multimedia software. However, sales promotion objectives and tools may need to be adjusted to accommodate a broader product line, a different target market, a different channel, and the rest of the promotion blend.

Price

Computer industry experts are predicting that retail prices for P.I.M. software will range from about $60 to $250—depending on the features of the software, the manufacturer, and the channel(s) in which it is distributed. This is a broad range of prices, but marketing research surveys suggest that there is also a broad range in the reference prices that different types of consumers give when they are asked what they would pay for P.I.M. software.

A wholesale price would need to be set taking into consideration costs, how channel markups will influence the final price, and how your target market would respond to that price. However, there is no reason to believe that your P.I.M. software has to be priced taking into consideratin the price level of your multimedia software. To the contrary, in other software product-markets, consumers have come to expect that firms may offer one product, say a wordprocessor, at a high price but another product, like a spreadsheet, at a low price.

Software dealers can be expected to stick to their customary markup percent. So traditional dealers in Channel 1 would use a 50 percent markup for P.I.M. software, and the limited-service dealers in Channel 2 would apply a 35 percent markup.

CUSTOMER CHOICES AMONG BRANDS

It's difficult to predict exactly how potential customers might react to one brand or another. But most customers will view this as an important decision. Thus, they will look for a product with features that meet their needs—at the right price.

Having the new product in the right place will certainly make a difference. Customers tend to shop for new software where they've purchased before—and, in some cases, the dealer's sales rep influences the decision.

The possibility of customers buying P.I.M. software from the producer of their multimedia software warrants special consideration. Certainly, brand awareness can make a difference when different brands are close substitutes. But experience in other software markets suggests that customers aren't very loyal to a particular software producer. They evaluate different products separately—and don't hesitate to buy different types of software from different producers. This can be good or bad—depending on your viewpoint. It means that you don't need to focus on the same target market for the two different products. On the other hand, it also means that your current strengths with a particular target market may not transfer to the new marketing mix.

MARKETING RESEARCH

Marketing research can help provide information about this new market opportunity. Your firm's marketing information system (MIS) and staff could certainly keep you informed of general developments in P.I.M. software, just as they do for multimedia software. In particular, the reports on industry sales, product features and prices, and marketing activity that you routinely receive should be updated to include information on P.I.M. software brands as they are introduced in the market.

In addition, the same outside research firm which provides the studies of the multimedia software market can provide similar studies for P.I.M. software. All of the same studies are available for P.I.M. software except report 6—Customer Shopping Habits Survey—which is not expected to differ for the new product. With one exception, costs for the reports are the same as for multimedia software. The exception is the Marketing Effectiveness Report (report 4) which will continue to cost $25,000 for one product—whether multimedia or P.I.M. software, or $30,000 if purchased for two products.

CONCLUSION

This report reviews a possible opportunity in the broad product-market in which you compete. It explains the changes that have led to that opportunity, provides some information about the needs of different segments of the broad market, and raises issues relevant to marketing mix planning.

Keep in mind, however, that important resource considerations are also relevant. Resources would be required to develop a successful product—and any additional marketing expenses would need to be considered relative to your firm's marketing budget. In other words—this is a decision that may require top management approval.

It appears there is a good opportunity here. However, there are also risks and some complications. Competitors' reactions and plans could be very important. We hope that this report provides a good base from which you can decide whether to pursue this opportunity—or instead devote your resources to doing a better job with your current markets.

Appendix A
Decision Support System

Note: Guided by inputs from the previous marketing manager, data processing specialists in the firm prepared an easy-to-use decision support system for the marketing department. This microcomputer software can be used to prepare an electronic version of the Marketing Plan Decision Form; it can also prepare a financial forecast (pro forma) for a marketing plan you are considering. This appendix is a set of instructions prepared by the data processing department on how to use the software.

The data processing department has developed a microcomputer program (decision support system), called PLAN, to make it easier to do marketing planning and evaluate the likely financial results (a pro forma) that might be achieved with alternative plans. The easy-to-use PLAN software—which is designed for use on IBM compatible microcomputers—also makes it easy to prepare an electronic version of the Marketing Plan Decision Form and to save it on a disk. The president may decide that you do not need to submit an electronic version of your plan along with the printed copy of your Marketing Plan Decision Form. And you can use the Budget Planning Form in Chapter 6—instead of the software—to prepare a pro forma. Thus, you may not need to use this software. But it is here if you want or need it.

These instructions explain how to setup and use the PLAN software. But, don't worry; you don't have to be a computer expert to use it. Even a real novice will find it quick and easy. And if you've already used a computer in the past, you may want to just go ahead and give the program a try (see the "fast start" instructions in the box below)—and read the instructions later. In fact, you may want to begin by experimenting with the software even if you have no previous experience. You can't hurt anything! And once you've tried the software you'll see that you won't need to worry much with memorizing directions here; after all, each screen asks the questions you should answer.

"Fast Start" Instructions for
People with Previous Computer Experience

1. Make a backup copy of the *Marketing Game* PLAN software disk that accompanies this manual; right your name, the letter for your industry, and your firm number on the label of the original disk.

2. Put the PLAN software disk in the disk drive on your computer; usually, it will be the A: drive. [Optionally, copy all of the files from the disk to a subdirectory on your hard drive.] At the DOS prompt, or in a Windows DOS box, make the disk drive (or subdirectory) where the software is located the default drive.

3. At the DOS prompt, type PLAN and press the enter key. Read the directions on the screens as they appear. Answer the questions by typing the appropriate response--like the letter Y for " yes" or N for "no" or a number to be filled in--at each shaded field on the screen. Use the number keys above the letters on the main keyboard to type numbers. Do not type commas when entering numbers, and enter only integers (whole numbers with no decimals). After you have filled in the value for one field, move to another field by pressing the enter key or the arrow keys. When you have double checked that *all* of the entries on a screen have been entered correctly, press the PgDn key to advance to the next screen. It's that simple. Skim Exhibit A2 for more information on using input screens.

4. The software will produce a file on your disk with the name INPUTS<u>if</u>.DAT (where i is replaced with the letter for your industry and f is replaced with the number for your firm). This file is the electronic version of your marketing plan. It can only be reviewed and modified with the PLAN software. It cannot be printed.

   If you ask for a pro forma, the software will also create a file named PROFORM<u>if</u>.TXT (where i is replaced with the letter for your industry and the last f is replaced with the number for your firm). This is a standard DOS (ASCII) format text file and can be reviewed or printed with almost any editor or wordprocessor. You can also use the DOS PRINT command to print the file.

5. The president of the firm will tell you whether or not you need to hand in the disk with the electronic version of your file. You will also be told if the disk is returned to you with a new file (your reports).

6. If these brief instructions are not clear to you, or if you have any questions about using the software, just look at the more detailed information that appears in the rest of the instructions.

Computer Requirements

The PLAN software is intended for use with an IBM PC, XT, AT, PS/1 or PS/2 computer or 100% IBM-compatible. Your computer must be running DOS version 2.0 or higher, Windows version 3.1 or higher, or OS/2 version 2.0 of higher; if you are using Windows or OS/2, see the notes at the end of this appendix. The software requires about 320K of available (free) RAM (memory). Memory resident ("TSR") programs may interfere with the operation of of the PLAN software. You can use the DOS VER command to find out what version of DOS you are using. You can use the DOS CHKDSK command to find out how much RAM memory you have available.

Running the PLAN Software

Start by putting the disk with the PLAN software in the disk drive of your computer. Usually, this will be the A: drive; if on your computer it is designated by some other letter, like B:, substitute that letter in the directions that follow. At the DOS prompt, type A: and press the enter key. This will make the A: drive your default drive.

- *Read this section only If you want to install the PLAN software on a harddrive.* We will assume that your harddrive is designated as the C: drive; if it is named with some other letter, substitute that letter instead.

  At the DOS prompt, type C: and press the enter key. This will make the C: harddrive your default drive. Then type CD C:\ and press enter. This will take you to the root directory on the harddrive. Next, type MD C:\TMG and press enter. This creates a subdirectory on the harddrive for the marketing game software. Then, type CD C:\TMG and press enter. This makes the TMG subdirectory on your harddrive the default directory.

  Next, type:
  ` COPY  A:*.*  C:\TMG  /V`
  and press enter. This will copy all of the files from your software disk to the \TMG subdirectory on your harddrive. Continue with the directions that follow. When we refer to the "default drive" below, we are refering the subdirectory on your harddrive where the PLAN software is stored.

At the DOS prompt (and with the default drive set to the drive where your PLAN software is stored), type
PLAN
and press the enter key. The computer will read the program from the disk drive, which takes a few seconds, a few technical messages will appear on the screen, and then a title screen will appear. Press the PgDn key to continue to the next screen, which will look like Exhibit A1.

Exhibit A1 - Firm Input Program Screen

```
          THE MARKETING GAME! Firm Input Program

  Use this program to input (or modify) plan decisions, compute
  a pro forma, and store decisions on a floppy disk.
  Before continuing, check that you have your completed
  decision form and a formated floppy disk to store the input file

  Please enter the LETTER code for your industry (A-Z): A
  Please enter the NUMBER code for your firm (1-4): 1
  Please enter the game level (1-3): 1

  Please specify the "path" where your input decision file will be
  saved.  Unless you change the path, your file will be saved to
  a disk in the A: drive.  Desired path: A:\

  Do you want to
   1:  Type in decisions from printed form.
   2:  Review and/or modify decision file.
   3:  Exit from the program.
  Type the number for your selection: 1

           Press [PgDn] when answers are correct....
```

You will notice that the screen provides instructions about what to do. In addition, on this screen and most of the others that follow you will fill in one or more blank fields before moving to the next screen. See Exhibit A2 on the next page for more information on using the input screens in the PLAN software.

On the initial screen, you will fill in several shaded input fields: one to specify the letter code for your industry, one for the number code for your firm, and one for the game level. If addition, if your plan file and/or pro forma file are somewhere other than on the disk in the A: drive, specify the path for the drive (and subdirectory). Next type the number that corresponds to what you want to do. Select 1 if you want to type in a new set of decisions from a printed form. This is usually the first step when you want to create an electronic version of the plan or prepare a pro forma report. If you have previously prepared a plan file, you can select 2 to review or modify the values from that file (and perhaps compute a modified pro forma based on the updated values). Or, if you want to exit the program and return to the DOS prompt, select 3.

When the input fields on the screen are correct, press the PgDn key again and you will move to the next screen. You will be instructed to insert a formatted disk in the default drive. If you want, you can just use your PLUS software disk, which is already inserted in the drive. Otherwise insert a some other formatted disk before pressing PgDn again.

This sequence will take you too a screen that looks like Exhibit A3; note that this is very similar in appearance to the printed Marketing Plan Decision Form; if you are instructed to develop plans that involve expanded marketing responsibilities (level 2 or level 3), the screens will look slightly different.

Exhibit A2--Using the Input Screens

The computer screens in the PLAN software are designed to be easy to use. In addition, most inputs are automatically checked to make certain that you are entering permissable values (which minimizes errors). For example, it is impossible to accidentally enter a negative price or to specific a firm number other than 1 through 4. Most screens contains one or more highlighted input fields. You will enter decisions in each highlighted field working from the upper left to the lower right on the screen. Below are some simple guidelines for using the screens:

1. Use the number keys above the letters on the main keyboard to type numbers.

2. Do NOT type in commas when entering numbers.

3. Type all numbers as integers--decimals are not permitted.

4. To enter a value into one field and move on to the next, type in the number(s) or letter(s) and press the enter key. The arrow keys will also move the cursor between fields.

5. To backup or return to a previous field, use the up arrow key; or, alternatively, press the enter key until you have cycled through all of the input fields and come back to the one of interest.

6. To "backspace" over what you have type in a field (say, to make a correction) before you have entered it, us the left arrow or the backspace.

7. If you hear the computer "beep," this means that you made an invalid entry. If this occurs, a message will appear at the bottom of the screen explaining the error. Backspace, and then type in a valid entry and continue.

8. When you have made all your inputs on the screen and have *checked* (!!!) that they are correct and what you intended, press the PgDn to continue with the program.

Exhibit A3—Level 1 Decision Screen

```
┌─INDUSTRY A ─────────── FIRM 1 ──────────────────────────────────┐
│                                      CHANNEL 1      CHANNEL 2    │
│    Number of Sales Reps:                10            10         │
│    Distribution Intensity (% of dealers):  30%        30%        │
│    Customer Service Budget:      $  92500                        │
│                                                                  │
│    Brand Name (10 characters):  FIRM X                           │
│    Brand Features:                                               │
│        Number of Special Commands:    8                          │
│        Error Protection:    3                                    │
│        Ease of Learning:    3                                    │
│    Production Order Quantity:     25000                          │
│                                                                  │
│    Advertising Dollars:  $  250000                               │
│                                                                  │
│    Wholesale Price:       $  95                                  │
│                                                                  │
│    Market Research Reports:  1  2  3  4  5  6                    │
│                              Y  Y  N  Y  Y  N                    │
├──────────────────────────────────────────────────────────────────┤
│    When all the data are input, press [PgDn] to continue.....    │
└──────────────────────────────────────────────────────────────────┘
```

On this screen, as with the printed form, you should fill in the shaded areas with the decision values for your plan. If you are typing in decisions from a printed form, the screen display a set of initial values provided by the program; if you are reviewing or modifying a (previously created) decision file, the initial values in the shaded fields will be the values from that file. In any event, change any field as necessary so that it is exactly what you want. It is very important to double check the entries for your decisions before you press PgDn to continue. Although the program checks entries to screen out some clerical errors, it can't read your mind. And a careless error on your part could cost your firm thousands. So play it safe and double check your work!

Once you move beyond the screen(s) to enter the values for your plan, you will be asked if you want a pro forma financial summary computed based on the plan values you have entered. It is a good idea to request and study the pro forma. Along with other calculations, the pro forma shows what expenses would be charged against your marketing budget with the current marketing plan. Clearly, you want to be certain that you are not planning a strategy that exceeds your available money. The pro form also shows what profit contribution might be expected from your plan—*if* you achieve the sales volume implied by your production request! Remember, though, that what sales you actually achieve will depend on many factors—so carefully forecasting is important to the accuracy of the pro forma.

If you request a pro forma, a new screen will appear that prompts you for several additional inputs that are needed to do the calculations. Specifically, the screen will request information about the levels of the product features from the previous period (needed to computed R&D for product modification costs), what percent of your sales you expect to come from each channel, and how many reps (if any) have been fired since the last period. You must enter the correct values for these items each time you compute a pro forma. Otherwise, product modification costs, firing costs, and perhaps other estimates will be based on inaccurate data. In other words, the PLAN software does not "track" the history of your previous decisions.

If you request a pro forma, it will be displayed on screen and look like Exhibit A4. Note that this format is very similar to the Budget Planning Form; thus, if you wish, you can complete the printed form from the results on the screen, or you can save the screen results as a computer file (which can subsequently be printed once you exit the PLAN software).

Exhibit A4—Sample of Pro Forma Screen

```
********* Industry A  Firm 1  Pro Forma Financial Summary *********
FIRM X                   Channel 1         Channel 2          Total
----------               ---------         ---------          -----
Est. Units Sold            12500             12500            25000
Wholesale Price              $95               $95
Base Unit C ost              $47               $47

Gross Sales              $1187500          $1187500         $2375000
Cost of Goods Sold        $587500           $587500         $1175000
Gross Margin                                                $1200000


Expenses
 Advertising                                                 $250000
 Sales Force - Salary     $200000           $200000          $400000
            - Firing Costs                                        $0
            - Commission    $59375            $59375          $118750
 Customer Service                                             $92500
 R&D for Product Modifications                                    $0
 Market Research                                              $67000
Total Expenses                                               $928250
Net Contribution (Loss)                                      $271750
         Total Spending Charged Against Budget:   $809500


                  Press [PgDn] to continue .....
            Display-only screen
```

There are no input fields on the pro forma display screen; thus, when you are finished reviewing the results all you need to do is press the PgDn key to continue. However, the next screen will give you the opportunity to "cycle back" through the decision inputs again to modify your decisions. That way, you can consider the financial implications of two or more alternative plans before making a final decision.

Each time you cycle through the PLAN software input screens it will create a new, updated decision file on your disk—and in the process replace the file for any previously entered decisions. Thus, if you are submitting a disk with an electronic version of your marketing plan decisions, be certain that the plan you want to submit is the last plan you entered in the PLAN software. **THIS IS VERY IMPORTANT**. Otherwise, you might mistakenly hand in a disk with the last plan that you evaluated—even if it is one you decided to reject.

Each time you ask for a pro forma from a set of plan decision values, the PLAN program stores the pro forma report on disk in a standard DOS format (ASCII) text file with the name PROFOR*if*, where the i is replaced with the letter for your industry and the f is replaced with the firm number.   Most popular word processing programs and most text editors (such as the DOS EDIT program) can read in this type file. Further, if you have a printer hooked to your computer that may be a convenient way to print the file. Alternatively, you should be able to print the file using whatever method you typically use to print a standard, 80 column wide text file. For example, one typical approach is to use the DOS PRINT command.

Using PLAN with Windows or OS/2

You should have no difficulty using the PLAN software with Windows or with OS/2. The simplest approach is to open a full-screen DOS session, and then just run the PLAN software by typing in the DOS statements described earlier in this appendix. However, if you wish, you can install the PLAN.BAT program with a icon on your OS/2 desktop or on your Windows program manager. Note, however, that this batch file executes a standard DOS program, and thus it is not a full-fledged Windows or OS/2 program and it doesn't comply with all of the conventions of these systems; for example, it will not respond to a mouse. Nevertheless, it is so simple to use that there is really no need for it to be able to do anything it doesn't do! At any rate, see your OS/2 or Windows documentation if you would like more details on how to open a full-screen DOS session or to install and run DOS software.

Index

THE MARKETING GAME! Decision Form
Level 1

Industry [ ]   **Firm** [ ]   **Period** [ ]

	Channel 1	Channel 2
Number of Sales Reps :	[ ]	[ ]
Distribution Intensity :	[%]	[%]

Customer Service: $ [   ]

Brand Name: [   ]

Brand Features:

Number of Special Commands (5 - 20): [   ]

Error Protection (1 - 10): [   ]

Ease of Learning (1 -10) : [   ]

Production Order Quantity: [   ]

Advertising Dollars : $ [   ]

Wholesale Price : $ [.00]

Marketing Research Reports (Y/N) :

1	2	3	4	5	6
[ ]	[ ]	[ ]	[ ]	[ ]	[ ]

Check here if exceptional items are noted on back of form: [ ]

Exceptional Items:

    Purchase of Additional Marketing Research: _____

    Fines: _____

    Budget Modifications: _____

Additional Information:

    _____

    _____

    _____

    _____

    _____

    _____

Signature of Firm's Representative: _____

Signature of Instructor: _____

Guide to Market Research Reports:
1. Market Share by Segment (all brands)
2. Market Share by Channel (all brands)
3. Consumer Preference Study
4. Marketing Effectiveness Report
5. Detailed Sales Analysis (own brand)
6. Customer Shopping Habits Study

THE MARKETING GAME! Decision Form
Level 1

Industry [ ]   Firm [ ]   Period [ ]

	Channel 1	Channel 2
Number of Sales Reps :	[ ]	[ ]
Distribution Intensity :	[ ] %	[ ] %

Customer Service: $ [ ]

Brand Name: [ ]

Brand Features:

Number of Special Commands (5 - 20): [ ]

Error Protection (1 - 10): [ ]

Ease of Learning (1 -10) : [ ]

Production Order Quantity: [ ]

Advertising Dollars : $ [ ]

Wholesale Price : $ [   ] .00

	1	2	3	4	5	6
Marketing Research Reports (Y/N) :	[ ]	[ ]	[ ]	[ ]	[ ]	[ ]

Check here if exceptional items are noted on back of form: [ ]

Exceptional Items:

   Purchase of Additional Marketing Research: _____

   Fines: _____

   Budget Modifications: _____

Additional Information:

_____

_____

_____

_____

_____

_____

Signature of Firm's Representative: _____

Signature of Instructor: _____

Guide to Market Research Reports:
1. Market Share by Segment (all brands)
2. Market Share by Channel (all brands)
3. Consumer Preference Study
4. Marketing Effectiveness Report
5. Detailed Sales Analysis (own brand)
6. Customer Shopping Habits Study

THE MARKETING GAME! Decision Form
Level 1

Industry [ ]   Firm [ ]   Period [ ]

	Channel 1	Channel 2
Number of Sales Reps :	[ ]	[ ]
Distribution Intensity :	[%]	[%]

Customer Service: $ [ ]

Brand Name: [ ]

Brand Features:

Number of Special Commands (5 - 20): [ ]

Error Protection (1 - 10): [ ]

Ease of Learning (1 -10) : [ ]

Production Order Quantity: [ ]

Advertising Dollars : $ [ ]

Wholesale Price : $ [.00]

	1	2	3	4	5	6
Marketing Research Reports (Y/N) :	[ ]	[ ]	[ ]	[ ]	[ ]	[ ]

Check here if exceptional items are noted on back of form: [ ]

Exceptional Items:

Purchase of Additional Marketing Research: _____

Fines: _____

Budget Modifications: _____

Additional Information:

_____

_____

_____

_____

_____

_____

Signature of Firm's Representative: _____

Signature of Instructor: _____

Guide to Market Research Reports:
1. Market Share by Segment (all brands)
2. Market Share by Channel (all brands)
3. Consumer Preference Study
4. Marketing Effectiveness Report
5. Detailed Sales Analysis (own brand)
6. Customer Shopping Habits Study

THE MARKETING GAME! Decision Form
Level 1

Industry [ ]   Firm [ ]   Period [ ]

	Channel 1	Channel 2
Number of Sales Reps :	[ ]	[ ]
Distribution Intensity :	[ ] %	[ ] %

Customer Service: $ [ ]

Brand Name: [ ]

Brand Features:

Number of Special Commands (5 - 20): [ ]

Error Protection (1 - 10): [ ]

Ease of Learning (1 -10) : [ ]

Production Order Quantity: [ ]

Advertising Dollars : $ [ ]

Wholesale Price : $ [ ] .00

	1	2	3	4	5	6
Marketing Research Reports (Y/N) :	[ ]	[ ]	[ ]	[ ]	[ ]	[ ]

Check here if exceptional items are noted on back of form: [ ]

Exceptional Items:

    Purchase of Additional Marketing Research: _____

    Fines: _____

    Budget Modifications: _____

Additional Information:

    _____

    _____

    _____

    _____

    _____

    _____

Signature of Firm's Representative: _____

Signature of Instructor: _____

Guide to Market Research Reports:

1. Market Share by Segment (all brands)
2. Market Share by Channel (all brands)
3. Consumer Preference Study
4. Marketing Effectiveness Report
5. Detailed Sales Analysis (own brand)
6. Customer Shopping Habits Study

THE MARKETING GAME! Decision Form
Level 1

Industry [ ]   Firm [ ]   Period [ ]

	Channel 1	Channel 2
Number of Sales Reps :	[ ]	[ ]
Distribution Intensity :	[%]	[%]
Customer Service:	$ [ ]	

Brand Name: [ ]

Brand Features:

Number of Special Commands (5 - 20): [ ]

Error Protection (1 - 10): [ ]

Ease of Learning (1 -10) : [ ]

Production Order Quantity: [ ]

Advertising Dollars : $ [ ]

Wholesale Price : $ [.00]

	1	2	3	4	5	6
Marketing Research Reports (Y/N) :	[ ]	[ ]	[ ]	[ ]	[ ]	[ ]

Check here if exceptional items are noted on back of form: [ ]

Exceptional Items:

Purchase of Additional Marketing Research: _____

Fines: _____

Budget Modifications: _____

Additional Information:

_____

_____

_____

_____

_____

_____

Signature of Firm's Representative: _____

Signature of Instructor: _____

Guide to Market Research Reports:
1. Market Share by Segment (all brands)
2. Market Share by Channel (all brands)
3. Consumer Preference Study
4. Marketing Effectiveness Report
5. Sales by Segment by Channel (own brand)
6. Consumer Shopping Habits Study
7. Product Positioning Report

Guide to Advertising Types:
P: Pioneering
D: Direct Competitive
I: Indirect Competitive
R: Reminder
C: Corporate or Institutional

THE MARKETING GAME! Decision Form
Level 1

Industry [ ]   Firm [ ]   Period [ ]

	Channel 1	Channel 2
Number of Sales Reps :	[ ]	[ ]
Distribution Intensity :	[%]	[%]

Customer Service: $ [ ]

Brand Name: [ ]

Brand Features:

Number of Special Commands (5 - 20): [ ]

Error Protection (1 - 10): [ ]

Ease of Learning (1 -10) : [ ]

Production Order Quantity: [ ]

Advertising Dollars : $ [ ]

Wholesale Price : $ [.00]

	1	2	3	4	5	6
Marketing Research Reports (Y/N) :	[ ]	[ ]	[ ]	[ ]	[ ]	[ ]

Check here if exceptional items are noted on back of form: [ ]

Exceptional Items:

    Purchase of Additional Marketing Research: _____

    Fines: _____

    Budget Modifications: _____

Additional Information:

    _____

    _____

    _____

    _____

    _____

    _____

Signature of Firm's Representative: _____

Signature of Instructor: _____

Guide to Market Research Reports:

1. Market Share by Segment (all brands)
2. Market Share by Channel (all brands)
3. Consumer Preference Study
4. Marketing Effectiveness Report
5. Detailed Sales Analysis (own brand)
6. Customer Shopping Habits Study

THE MARKETING GAME! Decision Form
Level 1

Industry [ ] **Firm** [ ] **Period** [ ]

	Channel 1	Channel 2
Number of Sales Reps :	[ ]	[ ]
Distribution Intensity :	[ ] %	[ ] %

Customer Service: $ [ ]

Brand Name: [ ]

Brand Features:

Number of Special Commands (5 - 20): [ ]

Error Protection (1 - 10): [ ]

Ease of Learning (1 -10) : [ ]

Production Order Quantity: [ ]

Advertising Dollars : $ [ ]

Wholesale Price : $ [ ] .00

	1	2	3	4	5	6
Marketing Research Reports (Y/N) :	[ ]	[ ]	[ ]	[ ]	[ ]	[ ]

Check here if exceptional items are noted on back of form: [ ]

Exceptional Items:

Purchase of Additional Marketing Research: _____

Fines: _____

Budget Modifications: _____

Additional Information:

_____

_____

_____

_____

_____

_____

Signature of Firm's Representative: _____

Signature of Instructor: _____

Guide to Market Research Reports:

1. Market Share by Segment (all brands)
2. Market Share by Channel (all brands)
3. Consumer Preference Study
4. Marketing Effectiveness Report
5. Detailed Sales Analysis (own brand)
6. Customer Shopping Habits Study

THE MARKETING GAME! Decision Form
Level 1

Industry [ ]   Firm [ ]   Period [ ]

	Channel 1	Channel 2
Number of Sales Reps :	[ ]	[ ]
Distribution Intensity :	[%]	[%]

Customer Service: $ [ ]

Brand Name: [ ]

Brand Features:

Number of Special Commands (5 - 20): [ ]

Error Protection (1 - 10): [ ]

Ease of Learning (1 -10) : [ ]

Production Order Quantity: [ ]

Advertising Dollars : $ [ ]

Wholesale Price : $ [.00]

Marketing Research Reports (Y/N) :   1 [ ] 2 [ ] 3 [ ] 4 [ ] 5 [ ] 6 [ ]

Check here if exceptional items are noted on back of form: [ ]

Exceptional Items:

Purchase of Additional Marketing Research: _____

Fines: _____

Budget Modifications: _____

Additional Information:

_____

_____

_____

_____

_____

_____

Signature of Firm's Representative: _____

Signature of Instructor: _____

Guide to Market Research Reports:

1. Market Share by Segment (all brands)
2. Market Share by Channel (all brands)
3. Consumer Preference Study
4. Marketing Effectiveness Report
5. Detailed Sales Analysis (own brand)
6. Customer Shopping Habits Study

THE MARKETING GAME! Decision Form
Level 2

Industry [ ]   Firm [ ]   Period [ ]

	Channel 1	Channel 2
Number of Sales Reps :	[ ]	[ ]
Distribution Intensity:	[%]	[%]
Percent Non-Selling Time (0 - 50) :	[%]	[%]

Sales Commission (0 - 15) : [%]

Customer Service: $ [ ]

Brand Name: [ ]

Brand Features:

Number of Special Commands (5 - 20): [ ]

Error Protection (1 - 10): [ ]

Ease of Learning (1 -10) : [ ]

Production Order Quantity: [ ]

Advertising Dollars : $ [ ]

Type of Advertising : [ ]
(P,D,I,R,C)

	Channel 1	Channel 2
Wholesale Prices :	$ [.00]	$ [.00]
Sales Promotion:	$ [ ]	$ [ ]

	1	2	3	4	5	6	7
Marketing Research Reports (Y/N) :	[ ]	[ ]	[ ]	[ ]	[ ]	[ ]	[ ]

Check here if exceptional items are noted on back of form: [ ]

Exceptional Items:

Purchase of Additional Marketing Research: _____

Fines: _____

Budget Modifications: _____

Additional Information:

_____

_____

_____

_____

_____

_____

Signature of Firm's Representative: _____

Signature of Instructor: _____

Guide to Market Research Reports:
1. Market Share by Segment (all brands)
2. Market Share by Channel (all brands)
3. Consumer Preference Study
4. Marketing Effectiveness Report
5. Detailed Sales Analysis (own brand)
6. Customer Shopping Habits Study

THE MARKETING GAME! Decision Form
Level 2

Industry [ ]   Firm [ ]   Period [ ]

	Channel 1	Channel 2
Number of Sales Reps :	[ ]	[ ]
Distribution Intensity:	[%]	[%]
Percent Non-Selling Time (0 - 50) :	[%]	[%]
Sales Commission (0 - 15) :	[%]	
Customer Service:	[$]	

Brand Name: [   ]

Brand Features:

Number of Special Commands (5 - 20): [ ]

Error Protection (1 - 10): [ ]

Ease of Learning (1 -10) : [ ]

Production Order Quantity: [   ]

Advertising Dollars : [$]

Type of Advertising : [ ]
(P,D,I,R,C)

	Channel 1	Channel 2
Wholesale Prices :	$ .00	$ .00
Sales Promotion:	$	$

	1	2	3	4	5	6	7
Marketing Research Reports (Y/N) :	[ ]	[ ]	[ ]	[ ]	[ ]	[ ]	[ ]

Check here if exceptional items are noted on back of form: [ ]

Exceptional Items:

Purchase of Additional Marketing Research: _____

Fines: _____

Budget Modifications: _____

Additional Information:

_____

_____

_____

_____

_____

_____

Signature of Firm's Representative: _____

Signature of Instructor: _____

Guide to Market Research Reports:

1. Market Share by Segment (all brands)
2. Market Share by Channel (all brands)
3. Consumer Preference Study
4. Marketing Effectiveness Report
5. Sales by Segment by Channel (own brand)
6. Consumer Shopping Habits Study
7. Product Positioning Report

Guide to Advertising Types:

P: Pioneering
D: Direct Competitive
I: Indirect Competitive
R: Reminder
C: Corporate or Institutional

THE MARKETING GAME! Decision Form
Level 2

Industry [ ]　　　**Firm** [ ]　　　**Period** [ ]

	Channel 1	Channel 2
Number of Sales Reps :	[ ]	[ ]
Distribution Intensity:	[%]	[%]
Percent Non-Selling Time (0 - 50) :	[%]	[%]
Sales Commission (0 - 15) :	[%]	
Customer Service:	[$]	

Brand Name: [ ]

Brand Features:

　Number of Special Commands (5 - 20): [ ]

　Error Protection (1 - 10): [ ]

　Ease of Learning (1 -10) : [ ]

Production Order Quantity: [ ]

Advertising Dollars : [$]

Type of Advertising : [ ]
(P,D,I,R,C)

	Channel 1	Channel 2
Wholesale Prices :	$ .00	$ .00
Sales Promotion:	$	$

	1	2	3	4	5	6	7
Marketing Research Reports (Y/N) :	[ ]	[ ]	[ ]	[ ]	[ ]	[ ]	[ ]

Check here if exceptional items are noted on back of form: [ ]

Exceptional Items:

Purchase of Additional Marketing Research: _____

Fines: _____

Budget Modifications: _____

Additional Information:

_____

_____

_____

_____

_____

_____

Signature of Firm's Representative: _____

Signature of Instructor: _____

Guide to Market Research Reports:
1. Market Share by Segment (all brands)
2. Market Share by Channel (all brands)
3. Consumer Preference Study
4. Marketing Effectiveness Report
5. Sales by Segment by Channel (own brand)
6. Consumer Shopping Habits Study
7. Product Positioning Report

Guide to Advertising Types:
P: Pioneering
D: Direct Competitive
I: Indirect Competitive
R: Reminder
C: Corporate or Institutional

THE MARKETING GAME! Decision Form
Level 2

Industry [ ]   **Firm** [ ]   **Period** [ ]

	Channel 1	Channel 2
Number of Sales Reps :	[ ]	[ ]
Distribution Intensity:	[%]	[%]
Percent Non-Selling Time (0 - 50) :	[%]	[%]

Sales Commission (0 - 15) : [%]

Customer Service: [$]

Brand Name: [ ]

Brand Features:

Number of Special Commands (5 - 20): [ ]

Error Protection (1 - 10): [ ]

Ease of Learning (1 -10) : [ ]

Production Order Quantity: [ ]

Advertising Dollars : [$]

Type of Advertising : [ ]
(P,D,I,R,C)

	Channel 1	Channel 2
Wholesale Prices :	[$ .00]	[$ .00]
Sales Promotion:	[$]	[$]

	1	2	3	4	5	6	7
Marketing Research Reports (Y/N) :	[ ]	[ ]	[ ]	[ ]	[ ]	[ ]	[ ]

Check here if exceptional items are noted on back of form: [ ]

Exceptional Items:

Purchase of Additional Marketing Research: _____

Fines: _____

Budget Modifications: _____

Additional Information:

_____

_____

_____

_____

_____

_____

Signature of Firm's Representative: _____

Signature of Instructor: _____

Guide to Market Research Reports:

1. Market Share by Segment (all brands)
2. Market Share by Channel (all brands)
3. Consumer Preference Study
4. Marketing Effectiveness Report
5. Sales by Segment by Channel (own brand)
6. Consumer Shopping Habits Study
7. Product Positioning Report

Guide to Advertising Types:

P: Pioneering
D: Direct Competitive
I: Indirect Competitive
R: Reminder
C: Corporate or Institutional

THE MARKETING GAME! Decision Form
Level 2

Industry [ ]　　　Firm [ ]　　　Period [ ]

	Channel 1	Channel 2
Number of Sales Reps :	[ ]	[ ]
Distribution Intensity:	[%]	[%]
Percent Non-Selling Time (0 - 50) :	[%]	[%]
Sales Commission (0 - 15) :	[%]	
Customer Service:	[$]	

Brand Name: [ ]

Brand Features:

Number of Special Commands (5 - 20): [ ]

Error Protection (1 - 10): [ ]

Ease of Learning (1 -10) : [ ]

Production Order Quantity: [ ]

Advertising Dollars : [$]

Type of Advertising : [ ]
(P,D,I,R,C)

	Channel 1	Channel 2
Wholesale Prices :	[$ .00]	[$ .00]
Sales Promotion:	[$]	[$]

Marketing Research Reports (Y/N) :

1	2	3	4	5	6	7
[ ]	[ ]	[ ]	[ ]	[ ]	[ ]	[ ]

Check here if exceptional items are noted on back of form: [ ]

Exceptional Items:

Purchase of Additional Marketing Research: _____

Fines: _____

Budget Modifications: _____

Additional Information:

_____

_____

_____

_____

_____

_____

Signature of Firm's Representative: _____

Signature of Instructor: _____

Guide to Market Research Reports:

1. Market Share by Segment (all brands)
2. Market Share by Channel (all brands)
3. Consumer Preference Study
4. Marketing Effectiveness Report
5. Sales by Segment by Channel (own brand)
6. Consumer Shopping Habits Study
7. Product Positioning Report

Guide to Advertising Types:

P: Pioneering
D: Direct Competitive
I: Indirect Competitive
R: Reminder
C: Corporate or Institutional

THE MARKETING GAME! Decision Form
Level 2

Industry [ ]   **Firm** [ ]   **Period** [ ]

	Channel 1	Channel 2
Number of Sales Reps :	[ ]	[ ]
Distribution Intensity:	[%]	[%]
Percent Non-Selling Time (0 - 50) :	[%]	[%]

Sales Commission (0 - 15) : [%]

Customer Service: [$]

Brand Name: [ ]

Brand Features:

   Number of Special Commands (5 - 20): [ ]

   Error Protection (1 - 10): [ ]

   Ease of Learning (1 -10) : [ ]

Production Order Quantity: [ ]

Advertising Dollars : [$]

Type of Advertising : [ ]
(P,D,I,R,C)

	Channel 1	Channel 2
Wholesale Prices :	[$ .00]	[$ .00]
Sales Promotion:	[$]	[$]

	1	2	3	4	5	6	7
Marketing Research Reports (Y/N) :	[ ]	[ ]	[ ]	[ ]	[ ]	[ ]	[ ]

Check here if exceptional items are noted on back of form: [ ]

Exceptional Items:

Purchase of Additional Marketing Research: _____

Fines: _____

Budget Modifications: _____

Additional Information:

_____

_____

_____

_____

_____

_____

Signature of Firm's Representative: _____

Signature of Instructor: _____

Guide to Market Research Reports:

1. Market Share by Segment (all brands)
2. Market Share by Channel (all brands)
3. Consumer Preference Study
4. Marketing Effectiveness Report
5. Sales by Segment by Channel (own brand)
6. Consumer Shopping Habits Study
7. Product Positioning Report

Guide to Advertising Types:

P: Pioneering
D: Direct Competitive
I: Indirect Competitive
R: Reminder
C: Corporate or Institutional

THE MARKETING GAME! Decision Form
Level 2

Industry [ ]   Firm [ ]   Period [ ]

	Channel 1	Channel 2
Number of Sales Reps :	[ ]	[ ]
Distribution Intensity:	[%]	[%]
Percent Non-Selling Time (0 - 50) :	[%]	[%]

Sales Commission (0 - 15) : [%]

Customer Service: $ [   ]

Brand Name: [   ]

Brand Features:

    Number of Special Commands (5 - 20): [ ]

    Error Protection (1 - 10): [ ]

    Ease of Learning (1 -10) : [ ]

Production Order Quantity: [   ]

Advertising Dollars : $ [   ]

Type of Advertising : [ ]
(P,D,I,R,C)

	Channel 1	Channel 2
Wholesale Prices :	$ .00	$ .00
Sales Promotion:	$	$

Marketing Research Reports (Y/N) :

1	2	3	4	5	6	7
[ ]	[ ]	[ ]	[ ]	[ ]	[ ]	[ ]

Check here if exceptional items are noted on back of form: [ ]

Exceptional Items:

    Purchase of Additional Marketing Research: _____

    Fines: _____

    Budget Modifications: _____

Additional Information:

_____

_____

_____

_____

_____

_____

Signature of Firm's Representative: _____

Signature of Instructor: _____

Guide to Market Research Reports:

1. Market Share by Segment (all brands)
2. Market Share by Channel (all brands)
3. Consumer Preference Study
4. Marketing Effectiveness Report
5. Sales by Segment by Channel (own brand)
6. Consumer Shopping Habits Study
7. Product Positioning Report

Guide to Advertising Types:

P: Pioneering
D: Direct Competitive
I: Indirect Competitive
R: Reminder
C: Corporate or Institutional

THE MARKETING GAME! Decision Form

Level 2

Industry [ ]   Firm [ ]   Period [ ]

	Channel 1	Channel 2
Number of Sales Reps :	[ ]	[ ]
Distribution Intensity:	[ ] %	[ ] %
Percent Non-Selling Time (0 - 50) :	[ ] %	[ ] %

Sales Commission (0 - 15) : [ ] %

Customer Service: $ [ ]

Brand Name: [ ]

Brand Features:

Number of Special Commands (5 - 20): [ ]

Error Protection (1 - 10): [ ]

Ease of Learning (1 -10) : [ ]

Production Order Quantity: [ ]

Advertising Dollars : $ [ ]

Type of Advertising : [ ]
(P,D,I,R,C)

	Channel 1	Channel 2
Wholesale Prices :	$ [.00]	$ [.00]
Sales Promotion:	$ [ ]	$ [ ]

Marketing Research Reports (Y/N) :

1	2	3	4	5	6	7
[ ]	[ ]	[ ]	[ ]	[ ]	[ ]	[ ]

Check here if exceptional items are noted on back of form: [ ]

Exceptional Items:

Purchase of Additional Marketing Research: _____

Fines: _____

Budget Modifications: _____

Additional Information:

_____

_____

_____

_____

_____

_____

Signature of Firm's Representative: _____

Signature of Instructor: _____

Guide to Market Research Reports:
1. Market Share by Segment (all brands)
2. Market Share by Channel (all brands)
3. Consumer Preference Study
4. Marketing Effectiveness Report
5. Sales by Segment by Channel (own brand)
6. Consumer Shopping Habits Study
7. Product Positioning Report

Guide to Advertising Types:
P: Pioneering
D: Direct Competitive
I: Indirect Competitive
R: Reminder
C: Corporate or Institutional

THE MARKETING GAME! Decision Form
Level 2

Industry [ ]   Firm [ ]   Period [ ]

	Channel 1	Channel 2
Number of Sales Reps :	[ ]	[ ]
Distribution Intensity:	[%]	[%]
Percent Non-Selling Time (0 - 50) :	[%]	[%]

Sales Commission (0 - 15) : [%]

Customer Service: [$]

Brand Name: [ ]

Brand Features:

  Number of Special Commands (5 - 20): [ ]

  Error Protection (1 - 10): [ ]

  Ease of Learning (1 -10) : [ ]

Production Order Quantity: [ ]

Advertising Dollars : [$]

Type of Advertising : [ ]
(P,D,I,R,C)

	Channel 1	Channel 2
Wholesale Prices :	$ .00	$ .00
Sales Promotion:	$	$

Marketing Research Reports (Y/N) :	1	2	3	4	5	6	7
	[ ]	[ ]	[ ]	[ ]	[ ]	[ ]	[ ]

Check here if exceptional items are noted on back of form: [ ]

Exceptional Items:

Purchase of Additional Marketing Research: _____

Fines: _____

Budget Modifications: _____

Additional Information:

_____

_____

_____

_____

_____

_____

Signature of Firm's Representative: _____

Signature of Instructor: _____

Guide to Market Research Reports:
1. Market Share by Segment (all brands)
2. Market Share by Channel (all brands)
3. Consumer Preference Study
4. Marketing Effectiveness Report
5. Sales by Segment by Channel (own brand)
6. Consumer Shopping Habits Study
7. Product Positioning Report

Guide to Advertising Types:
P: Pioneering
D: Direct Competitive
I: Indirect Competitive
R: Reminder
C: Corporate or Institutional

THE MARKETING GAME! Decision Form
Level 2

Industry [   ]   **Firm** [   ]   **Period** [   ]

	Channel 1	Channel 2
Number of Sales Reps :	[ ]	[ ]
Distribution Intensity:	[%]	[%]
Percent Non-Selling Time (0 - 50) :	[%]	[%]

Sales Commission (0 - 15) : [%]

Customer Service: [$]

Brand Name: [   ]

Brand Features:

Number of Special Commands (5 - 20): [   ]

Error Protection (1 - 10): [   ]

Ease of Learning (1 -10) : [   ]

Production Order Quantity: [   ]

Advertising Dollars : [$]

Type of Advertising : [   ]
(P,D,I,R,C)

	Channel 1	Channel 2
Wholesale Prices :	$ .00	$ .00
Sales Promotion:	$	$

Marketing Research Reports (Y/N) :

1	2	3	4	5	6	7
[ ]	[ ]	[ ]	[ ]	[ ]	[ ]	[ ]

Check here if exceptional items are noted on back of form: [   ]

Exceptional Items:

    Purchase of Additional Marketing Research: _____

    Fines: _____

    Budget Modifications: _____

Additional Information:

    _____

    _____

    _____

    _____

    _____

    _____

Signature of Firm's Representative: _____

Signature of Instructor: _____

Guide to Market Research Reports:
1. Market Share by Segment (all brands)
2. Market Share by Channel (all brands)
3. Consumer Preference Study
4. Marketing Effectiveness Report
5. Sales by Segment by Channel (own brand)
6. Consumer Shopping Habits Study
7. Product Positioning Report

Guide to Advertising Types:
P: Pioneering
D: Direct Competitive
I: Indirect Competitive
R: Reminder
C: Corporate or Institutional

THE MARKETING GAME! Decision Form

Level 3

Industry [   ]   **Firm** [   ]   **Period** [   ]

	Channel 1	Channel 2
Number of Sales Reps :	[ ]	[ ]
Distribution Intensity:	[ ]%	[ ]%
Percent Non-Selling Time (0 - 50) :	[ ]%	[ ]%
Sales Commission (0 - 15) :	[ ]%	
Customer Service:	$ [ ]	

PRODUCT 1:   Brand Name: [   ]

Brand Features:

Number of Special Commands (5 - 20): [   ]

Error Protection (1 - 10): [   ]

Ease of Learning (1 -10) : [   ]

Production Order Quantity: [   ]

Advertising Dollars : $ [   ]

Type of Advertising : [   ]
(P,D,I,R,C)

	Channel 1	Channel 2
Wholesale Prices :	$ [ ].00	$ [ ].00
Sales Promotion:	$ [ ]	$ [ ]

Marketing Research Reports (Y/N) :	1	2	3	4	5	6	7
	[ ]	[ ]	[ ]	[ ]	[ ]	[ ]	[ ]

Complete other side for second product. . .

THE MARKETING GAME! Decision Form
Level 3

PRODUCT 2:

Brand Name : [ ]

Brand Features:

Number of Tasks (1 - 10): [ ]

Similarity of Commands (1 - 10): [ ]

Ability to Customize (1 -10) : [ ]

Production Order Quantity: [ ]

Advertising Dollars : $ [ ]

Type of Advertising : [ ]
(P,D,I,R,C)

	Channel 1	Channel 2
Wholesale Prices :	$ .00	$ .00
Sales Promotion:	$	$

Marketing Research Reports (Y/N) :

1	2	3	4	5	6	7
[ ]	[ ]	[ ]	[ ]	[ ]	N/A	[ ]

Exceptional Items:

Additional Marketing Research: _____

Fines: _____

Budget Modifications: _____

Signature of Firm's Representative: _____

Signature of Instructor: _____

THE MARKETING GAME! Decision Form

Level 3

Industry [ ]   **Firm** [ ]   **Period** [ ]

	Channel 1	Channel 2
Number of Sales Reps :	[ ]	[ ]
Distribution Intensity:	[%]	[%]
Percent Non-Selling Time (0 - 50) :	[%]	[%]
Sales Commission (0 - 15) :	[%]	
Customer Service:	[$]	

__PRODUCT 1:__   Brand Name: [ ]

Brand Features:
- Number of Special Commands (5 - 20): [ ]
- Error Protection (1 - 10): [ ]
- Ease of Learning (1 -10) : [ ]

Production Order Quantity: [ ]

Advertising Dollars : [$]

Type of Advertising : [ ]
(P,D,I,R,C)

	Channel 1	Channel 2
Wholesale Prices :	$ .00	$ .00
Sales Promotion:	$	$

Marketing Research Reports (Y/N) :	1	2	3	4	5	6	7
	[ ]	[ ]	[ ]	[ ]	[ ]	[ ]	[ ]

Complete other side for second product. . .

THE MARKETING GAME! Decision Form
Level 3

PRODUCT 2:

Brand Name :

Brand Features:

Number of Tasks (1 - 10):

Similarity of Commands (1 - 10):

Ability to Customize (1 -10) :

Production Order Quantity:

Advertising Dollars : $

Type of Advertising :

(P,D,I,R,C)

	Channel 1	Channel 2
Wholesale Prices :	$ .00	$ .00
Sales Promotion:	$	$

Marketing Research Reports (Y/N) :

1	2	3	4	5	6	7
					N/A	

Exceptional Items:

Additional Marketing Research: _____

Fines: _____

Budget Modifications: _____

Signature of Firm's Representative:_____

Signature of Instructor: _____

THE MARKETING GAME! Decision Form

Level 3

Industry [ ]   **Firm** [ ]   **Period** [ ]

	Channel 1	Channel 2
Number of Sales Reps :	[ ]	[ ]
Distribution Intensity:	[%]	[%]
Percent Non-Selling Time (0 - 50) :	[%]	[%]
Sales Commission (0 - 15) :	[%]	
Customer Service:	[$]	

PRODUCT 1:   Brand Name: [ ]

Brand Features:

Number of Special Commands (5 - 20): [ ]

Error Protection (1 - 10): [ ]

Ease of Learning (1 -10) : [ ]

Production Order Quantity: [ ]

Advertising Dollars : [$]

Type of Advertising : [ ]
(P,D,I,R,C)

	Channel 1	Channel 2
Wholesale Prices :	$ .00	$ .00
Sales Promotion:	$	$

Marketing Research Reports (Y/N) :	1	2	3	4	5	6	7
	[ ]	[ ]	[ ]	[ ]	[ ]	[ ]	[ ]

Complete other side for second product. . .

THE MARKETING GAME! Decision Form
Level 3

PRODUCT 2:

Brand Name : _____

Brand Features:
Number of Tasks (1 - 10): ___

Similarity of Commands (1 - 10): ___

Ability to Customize (1 -10) : ___

Production Order Quantity: _____

Advertising Dollars : $ _____

Type of Advertising : ___
(P,D,I,R,C)

	Channel 1	Channel 2
Wholesale Prices :	$ .00	$ .00
Sales Promotion:	$	$

Marketing Research Reports (Y/N) :

1	2	3	4	5	6	7
☐	☐	☐	☐	☐	N/A	☐

Exceptional Items:

Additional Marketing Research: _____

Fines: _____

Budget Modifications: _____

Signature of Firm's Representative: _____

Signature of Instructor: _____

THE MARKETING GAME! Decision Form

Level 3

Industry [ ]   **Firm** [ ]   **Period** [ ]

	Channel 1	Channel 2
Number of Sales Reps :	[ ]	[ ]
Distribution Intensity:	[%]	[%]
Percent Non-Selling Time (0 - 50) :	[%]	[%]
Sales Commission (0 - 15) :	[%]	
Customer Service:	$ [ ]	

PRODUCT 1:   Brand Name: [ ]

Brand Features:

Number of Special Commands (5 - 20): [ ]

Error Protection (1 - 10): [ ]

Ease of Learning (1 -10) : [ ]

Production Order Quantity: [ ]

Advertising Dollars : $ [ ]

Type of Advertising : [ ]
(P,D,I,R,C)

	Channel 1	Channel 2
Wholesale Prices :	$ [ ].00	$ [ ].00
Sales Promotion:	$ [ ]	$ [ ]

Marketing Research Reports (Y/N) :

1	2	3	4	5	6	7
[ ]	[ ]	[ ]	[ ]	[ ]	[ ]	[ ]

Complete other side for second product. . .

THE MARKETING GAME! Decision Form
Level 3

PRODUCT 2:

Brand Name :

Brand Features:
   Number of Tasks (1 - 10):

   Similarity of Commands (1 - 10):

   Ability to Customize (1 -10) :

Production Order Quantity:

Advertising Dollars : $

Type of Advertising :
   (P,D,I,R,C)

	Channel 1	Channel 2
Wholesale Prices :	$ .00	$ .00
Sales Promotion:	$	$

Marketing Research Reports (Y/N) :

	1	2	3	4	5	6	7
						N/A	

Exceptional Items:

   Additional Marketing Research: _____

   Fines: _____

   Budget Modifications: _____

Signature of Firm's Representative:_____

Signature of Instructor: _____

THE MARKETING GAME! Decision Form

Level 3

Industry [ ] **Firm** [ ] **Period** [ ]

	Channel 1	Channel 2
Number of Sales Reps :	[ ]	[ ]
Distribution Intensity:	[%]	[%]
Percent Non-Selling Time (0 - 50) :	[%]	[%]
Sales Commission (0 - 15) :	[%]	
Customer Service:	$ [ ]	

PRODUCT 1:   Brand Name: [ ]

Brand Features:

Number of Special Commands (5 - 20): [ ]

Error Protection (1 - 10): [ ]

Ease of Learning (1 -10) : [ ]

Production Order Quantity: [ ]

Advertising Dollars : $ [ ]

Type of Advertising : [ ]
(P,D,I,R,C)

	Channel 1	Channel 2
Wholesale Prices :	$ [.00]	$ [.00]
Sales Promotion:	$ [ ]	$ [ ]

Marketing Research Reports (Y/N) :

1	2	3	4	5	6	7
[ ]	[ ]	[ ]	[ ]	[ ]	[ ]	[ ]

Complete other side for second product. . .

THE MARKETING GAME! Decision Form
Level 3

PRODUCT 2:

Brand Name :

Brand Features:
    Number of Tasks (1 - 10):

    Similarity of Commands (1 - 10):

    Ability to Customize (1 -10) :

Production Order Quantity:

Advertising Dollars : $

Type of Advertising :
    (P,D,I,R,C)

	Channel 1	Channel 2
Wholesale Prices :	$ .00	$ .00
Sales Promotion:	$	$

Marketing Research Reports (Y/N) :   1 2 3 4 5 6 N/A 7

Exceptional Items:

    Additional Marketing Research: _____

    Fines: _____

    Budget Modifications: _____

Signature of Firm's Representative: _____

Signature of Instructor: _____

THE MARKETING GAME! Decision Form

Level 3

Industry [ ]   **Firm** [ ]   **Period** [ ]

	Channel 1	Channel 2
Number of Sales Reps :	[ ]	[ ]
Distribution Intensity:	[%]	[%]
Percent Non-Selling Time (0 - 50) :	[%]	[%]
Sales Commission (0 - 15) :	[%]	
Customer Service:	[$]	

PRODUCT 1:   Brand Name: [   ]

Brand Features:

Number of Special Commands (5 - 20): [ ]

Error Protection (1 - 10): [ ]

Ease of Learning (1 -10) : [ ]

Production Order Quantity: [ ]

Advertising Dollars : [$]

Type of Advertising : [ ]
(P,D,I,R,C)

	Channel 1	Channel 2
Wholesale Prices :	$ .00	$ .00
Sales Promotion:	$	$

	1	2	3	4	5	6	7
Marketing Research Reports (Y/N) :	[ ]	[ ]	[ ]	[ ]	[ ]	[ ]	[ ]

Complete other side for second product. . .

THE MARKETING GAME! Decision Form
Level 3

PRODUCT 2:

Brand Name : _____

Brand Features:

Number of Tasks (1 - 10): ☐

Similarity of Commands (1 - 10): ☐

Ability to Customize (1 -10) : ☐

Production Order Quantity: _____

Advertising Dollars : $_____

Type of Advertising : ☐
(P,D,I,R,C)

	Channel 1	Channel 2
Wholesale Prices :	$_____.00	$_____.00
Sales Promotion:	$_____	$_____

Marketing Research Reports (Y/N) :

1	2	3	4	5	6	7
☐	☐	☐	☐	☐	N/A	☐

Exceptional Items:

Additional Marketing Research: _____

Fines: _____

Budget Modifications: _____

Signature of Firm's Representative:_____

Signature of Instructor: _____

THE MARKETING GAME! Decision Form

Level 3

Industry [   ]　　Firm [   ]　　Period [   ]

Number of Sales Reps :

	Channel 1	Channel 2
Number of Sales Reps :	[ ]	[ ]
Distribution Intensity:	[ ] %	[ ] %
Percent Non-Selling Time (0 - 50) :	[ ] %	[ ] %

Sales Commission (0 - 15) : [   ] %

Customer Service: $ [   ]

PRODUCT 1:　　Brand Name: [   ]

Brand Features:

Number of Special Commands (5 - 20): [   ]

Error Protection (1 - 10): [   ]

Ease of Learning (1 -10) : [   ]

Production Order Quantity: [   ]

Advertising Dollars : $ [   ]

Type of Advertising : [   ]
(P,D,I,R,C)

	Channel 1	Channel 2
Wholesale Prices :	$ [ ] .00	$ [ ] .00
Sales Promotion:	$ [ ]	$ [ ]

	1	2	3	4	5	6	7
Marketing Research Reports (Y/N) :	[ ]	[ ]	[ ]	[ ]	[ ]	[ ]	[ ]

Complete other side for second product. . .

THE MARKETING GAME! Decision Form
Level 3

PRODUCT 2:

Brand Name :

Brand Features:
    Number of Tasks (1 - 10):

    Similarity of Commands (1 - 10):

    Ability to Customize (1 -10) :

Production Order Quantity:

Advertising Dollars : $

Type of Advertising :
    (P,D,I,R,C)

	Channel 1	Channel 2
Wholesale Prices :	$ .00	$ .00
Sales Promotion:	$	$

Marketing Research Reports (Y/N) :

1	2	3	4	5	6	7
					N/A	

Exceptional Items:
    Additional Marketing Research: _____

    Fines: _____

    Budget Modifications: _____

Signature of Firm's Representative:_____

Signature of Instructor: _____

THE MARKETING GAME! Decision Form

Level 3

Industry [ ]   **Firm** [ ]   **Period** [ ]

	Channel 1	Channel 2
Number of Sales Reps :	[ ]	[ ]
Distribution Intensity:	[%]	[%]
Percent Non-Selling Time (0 - 50) :	[%]	[%]
Sales Commission (0 - 15) :	[%]	
Customer Service:	$ [ ]	

PRODUCT 1:   Brand Name: [ ]

Brand Features:

Number of Special Commands (5 - 20): [ ]

Error Protection (1 - 10): [ ]

Ease of Learning (1 -10) : [ ]

Production Order Quantity: [ ]

Advertising Dollars : $ [ ]

Type of Advertising : [ ]
(P,D,I,R,C)

	Channel 1	Channel 2
Wholesale Prices :	$ .00	$ .00
Sales Promotion:	$ [ ]	$ [ ]

	1	2	3	4	5	6	7
Marketing Research Reports (Y/N) :	[ ]	[ ]	[ ]	[ ]	[ ]	[ ]	[ ]

Complete other side for second product. . .

THE MARKETING GAME! Decision Form
Level 3

PRODUCT 2:

Brand Name :

Brand Features:

Number of Tasks (1 - 10):

Similarity of Commands (1 - 10):

Ability to Customize (1 -10) :

Production Order Quantity:

Advertising Dollars : $

Type of Advertising :
(P,D,I,R,C)

	Channel 1	Channel 2
Wholesale Prices :	$ .00	$ .00
Sales Promotion:	$	$

Marketing Research Reports (Y/N) :

1	2	3	4	5	6	7
					N/A	

Exceptional Items:

Additional Marketing Research: _____

Fines: _____

Budget Modifications: _____

Signature of Firm's Representative:_____

Signature of Instructor: _____

THE MARKETING GAME! Decision Form

Level 3

Industry [ ]   **Firm** [ ]   **Period** [ ]

	Channel 1	Channel 2
Number of Sales Reps :	[ ]	[ ]
Distribution Intensity:	[%]	[%]
Percent Non-Selling Time (0 - 50) :	[%]	[%]
Sales Commission (0 - 15) :	[%]	
Customer Service:	[$]	

PRODUCT 1:   Brand Name: [ ]

Brand Features:

Number of Special Commands (5 - 20): [ ]

Error Protection (1 - 10): [ ]

Ease of Learning (1 -10) : [ ]

Production Order Quantity: [ ]

Advertising Dollars : [$]

Type of Advertising : [ ]
(P,D,I,R,C)

	Channel 1	Channel 2
Wholesale Prices :	$ .00	$ .00
Sales Promotion:	$	$

Marketing Research Reports (Y/N) :	1	2	3	4	5	6	7
	[ ]	[ ]	[ ]	[ ]	[ ]	[ ]	[ ]

Complete other side for second product. . .

THE MARKETING GAME! Decision Form
Level 3

PRODUCT 2:

Brand Name : [   ]

Brand Features:

    Number of Tasks (1 - 10): [   ]

    Similarity of Commands (1 - 10): [   ]

    Ability to Customize (1 -10) : [   ]

Production Order Quantity: [   ]

Advertising Dollars : $ [   ]

Type of Advertising : [   ]
    (P,D,I,R,C)

	Channel 1	Channel 2
Wholesale Prices :	$ .00	$ .00
Sales Promotion:	$	$

Marketing Research Reports (Y/N) :

1	2	3	4	5	6	7
[ ]	[ ]	[ ]	[ ]	[ ]	N/A	[ ]

Exceptional Items:

    Additional Marketing Research: _____

    Fines: _____

    Budget Modifications: _____

Signature of Firm's Representative:_____

Signature of Instructor: _____

THE MARKETING GAME! Decision Form

Level 3

Industry [ ] **Firm** [ ] **Period** [ ]

	Channel 1	Channel 2
Number of Sales Reps :	[ ]	[ ]
Distribution Intensity:	[%]	[%]
Percent Non-Selling Time (0 - 50) :	[%]	[%]
Sales Commission (0 - 15) :	[%]	
Customer Service:	$ [ ]	

PRODUCT 1:   Brand Name: [ ]

Brand Features:

Number of Special Commands (5 - 20): [ ]

Error Protection (1 - 10): [ ]

Ease of Learning (1 -10) : [ ]

Production Order Quantity: [ ]

Advertising Dollars : $ [ ]

Type of Advertising : [ ]
(P,D,I,R,C)

	Channel 1	Channel 2
Wholesale Prices :	$ .00	$ .00
Sales Promotion:	$ [ ]	$ [ ]

Marketing Research Reports (Y/N) :	1	2	3	4	5	6	7
	[ ]	[ ]	[ ]	[ ]	[ ]	[ ]	[ ]

Complete other side for second product. . .

THE MARKETING GAME! Decision Form
Level 3

PRODUCT 2:

Brand Name :

Brand Features:

Number of Tasks (1 - 10):

Similarity of Commands (1 - 10):

Ability to Customize (1 -10) :

Production Order Quantity:

Advertising Dollars : $

Type of Advertising :
(P,D,I,R,C)

	Channel 1	Channel 2
Wholesale Prices :	$ .00	$ .00
Sales Promotion:	$	$

	1	2	3	4	5	6	7
Marketing Research Reports (Y/N) :						N/A	

Exceptional Items:

Additional Marketing Research: _____

Fines: _____

Budget Modifications: _____

Signature of Firm's Representative: _____

Signature of Instructor: _____

BUDGET PLANNING FORM for The Marketing Game!

```
******Financial Summary / Pro Forma ******
```

Industry: _____ Firm: _____ Period: _____ Brandname: _____

	Channel 1	Channel 2	Total
(1) **Estimated Units Sold**	_____	_____	_____
(2) **Wholesale Price**	$_____	$_____	
(3) **Base Unit Cost**	$_____	$_____	
(4) **Gross Sales** [(1) × (2)]	$_____	$_____	$_____
(5) **Cost of Goods Sold** [(1) × (3)]	$_____	$_____	$_____
(6) **GROSS MARGIN** [(4) minus (5)]			$_____

EXPENSES:

	Channel 1	Channel 2	Total
(7) **Advertising**			$_____
(8) **Sales Force-Salary**	$_____	$_____	$_____
(9) **Sales Force-Firing Costs**	$_____	$_____	$_____
(10) **Sales Force-Commission**	$_____	$_____	$_____
(11) **Customer Service**			$_____
(12) **Sales Promotion**	$_____	$_____	$_____
(13) **R&D for Product Modification**			$_____
(14) **Marketing Research**			$_____
(15) **TOTAL EXPENSES** [sum of (7) to (14)]			$_____
(16) **Net Contribution to Profit or Loss** [(6) minus (15)]			$_____
(17) **Total Spending against Budget** [(15) minus (10)]			$_____

Strategy Summary Form - The Marketing Game!

Industry: _____   Firm: _____   Period: _____

Target Market(s): _____
_____
_____
_____

Product: _____
_____
_____
_____

Place: _____
_____
_____
_____

Promotion: _____
_____
_____
_____

Price: _____
_____
_____
_____

Competition: _____
_____
_____
_____
_____
_____

BUDGET PLANNING FORM for The Marketing Game!

******Financial Summary / Pro Forma ******

Industry: _____ Firm: _____ Period: _____ Brandname: _____

	Channel 1	Channel 2	Total
(1) Estimated Units Sold	_____	_____	_____
(2) Wholesale Price	$_____	$_____	
(3) Base Unit Cost	$_____	$_____	
(4) Gross Sales [(1) ×(2)]	$_____	$_____	$_____
(5) Cost of Goods Sold [(1) × (3)]	$_____	$_____	$_____
(6) GROSS MARGIN [(4) minus (5)]			$_____

EXPENSES:

	Channel 1	Channel 2	Total
(7) Advertising			$_____
(8) Sales Force-Salary	$_____	$_____	$_____
(9) Sales Force-Firing Costs	$_____	$_____	$_____
(10) Sales Force-Commission	$_____	$_____	$_____
(11) Customer Service			$_____
(12) Sales Promotion	$_____	$_____	$_____
(13) R&D for Product Modification			$_____
(14) Marketing Research			$_____
(15) TOTAL EXPENSES [sum of (7) to (14)]			$_____
(16) Net Contribution to Profit or Loss [(6) minus (15)]			$_____
(17) Total Spending against Budget [(15) minus (10)]			$_____

Strategy Summary Form - The Marketing Game!

Industry: _____   Firm: _____   Period: _____

Target Market(s): _____
_____
_____
_____

Product: _____
_____
_____
_____

Place: _____
_____
_____
_____

Promotion: _____
_____
_____
_____

Price: _____
_____
_____
_____

Competition: _____
_____
_____
_____
_____
_____

BUDGET PLANNING FORM for The Marketing Game!

******Financial Summary / Pro Forma ******

Industry: _____ Firm: _____ Period: _____ Brandname: _____

	Channel 1	Channel 2	Total
(1) Estimated Units Sold	_____	_____	_____
(2) Wholesale Price	$_____	$_____	
(3) Base Unit Cost	$_____	$_____	
(4) Gross Sales [(1) × (2)]	$_____	$_____	$_____
(5) Cost of Goods Sold [(1) × (3)]	$_____	$_____	$_____
(6) GROSS MARGIN [(4) minus (5)]			$_____

EXPENSES:

	Channel 1	Channel 2	Total
(7) Advertising			$_____
(8) Sales Force-Salary	$_____	$_____	$_____
(9) Sales Force-Firing Costs	$_____	$_____	$_____
(10) Sales Force-Commission	$_____	$_____	$_____
(11) Customer Service			$_____
(12) Sales Promotion	$_____	$_____	$_____
(13) R&D for Product Modification			$_____
(14) Marketing Research			$_____
(15) TOTAL EXPENSES [sum of (7) to (14)]			$_____
(16) Net Contribution to Profit or Loss [(6) minus (15)]			$_____
(17) Total Spending against Budget [(15) minus (10)]			$_____

Strategy Summary Form - The Marketing Game!

Industry: _____   Firm: _____   Period: _____

Target Market(s): _____
_____
_____
_____

Product: _____
_____
_____
_____

Place: _____
_____
_____
_____

Promotion: _____
_____
_____
_____

Price: _____
_____
_____
_____

Competition: _____
_____
_____
_____
_____
_____

BUDGET PLANNING FORM for The Marketing Game!

******Financial Summary / Pro Forma ******

Industry: _____ Firm: _____ Period: _____ Brandname: _____

	Channel 1	Channel 2	Total
(1) Estimated Units Sold	_____	_____	_____
(2) Wholesale Price	$_____	$_____	
(3) Base Unit Cost	$_____	$_____	
(4) Gross Sales [(1) × (2)]	$_____	$_____	$_____
(5) Cost of Goods Sold [(1) × (3)]	$_____	$_____	$_____
(6) GROSS MARGIN [(4) minus (5)]			$_____

EXPENSES:

	Channel 1	Channel 2	Total
(7) Advertising			$_____
(8) Sales Force-Salary	$_____	$_____	$_____
(9) Sales Force-Firing Costs	$_____	$_____	$_____
(10) Sales Force-Commission	$_____	$_____	$_____
(11) Customer Service			$_____
(12) Sales Promotion	$_____	$_____	$_____
(13) R&D for Product Modification			$_____
(14) Marketing Research			$_____
(15) TOTAL EXPENSES [sum of (7) to (14)]			$_____
(16) Net Contribution to Profit or Loss [(6) minus (15)]			$_____
(17) Total Spending against Budget [(15) minus (10)]			$_____

Strategy Summary Form - The Marketing Game!

Industry: _____   Firm: _____   Period: _____

Target Market(s): _____
_____
_____
_____

Product: _____
_____
_____
_____

Place: _____
_____
_____
_____

Promotion: _____
_____
_____
_____

Price: _____
_____
_____
_____

Competition: _____
_____
_____
_____
_____
_____

BUDGET PLANNING FORM for The Marketing Game!

******Financial Summary / Pro Forma ******

Industry: ____ Firm: ____ Period: ____ Brandname: _____

	Channel 1	Channel 2	Total
(1) Estimated Units Sold	_____	_____	_____
(2) Wholesale Price	$_____	$_____	
(3) Base Unit Cost	$_____	$_____	
(4) Gross Sales [(1) × (2)]	$_____	$_____	$_____
(5) Cost of Goods Sold [(1) × (3)]	$_____	$_____	$_____
(6) GROSS MARGIN [(4) minus (5)]			$_____

EXPENSES:

	Channel 1	Channel 2	Total
(7) Advertising			$_____
(8) Sales Force-Salary	$_____	$_____	$_____
(9) Sales Force-Firing Costs	$_____	$_____	$_____
(10) Sales Force-Commission	$_____	$_____	$_____
(11) Customer Service			$_____
(12) Sales Promotion	$_____	$_____	$_____
(13) R&D for Product Modification			$_____
(14) Marketing Research			$_____
(15) TOTAL EXPENSES [sum of (7) to (14)]			$_____
(16) Net Contribution to Profit or Loss [(6) minus (15)]			$_____
(17) Total Spending against Budget [(15) minus (10)]			$_____

Strategy Summary Form - The Marketing Game!

Industry: _____   Firm: _____   Period: ____

Target Market(s): _____
_____
_____
_____

Product: _____
_____
_____
_____

Place: _____
_____
_____
_____

Promotion: _____
_____
_____
_____

Price: _____
_____
_____
_____

Competition: _____
_____
_____
_____
_____
_____

BUDGET PLANNING FORM for The Marketing Game!

```
******Financial Summary / Pro Forma ******
```

Industry: _____ Firm: _____ Period: _____ Brandname: _____

	Channel 1	Channel 2	Total
(1) Estimated Units Sold	_____	_____	_____
(2) Wholesale Price	$_____	$_____	
(3) Base Unit Cost	$_____	$_____	
(4) Gross Sales [(1) × (2)]	$_____	$_____	$_____
(5) Cost of Goods Sold [(1) × (3)]	$_____	$_____	$_____
(6) GROSS MARGIN [(4) minus (5)]			$_____

EXPENSES:

	Channel 1	Channel 2	Total
(7) Advertising			$_____
(8) Sales Force-Salary	$_____	$_____	$_____
(9) Sales Force-Firing Costs	$_____	$_____	$_____
(10) Sales Force-Commission	$_____	$_____	$_____
(11) Customer Service			$_____
(12) Sales Promotion	$_____	$_____	$_____
(13) R&D for Product Modification			$_____
(14) Marketing Research			$_____
(15) TOTAL EXPENSES [sum of (7) to (14)]			$_____
(16) Net Contribution to Profit or Loss [(6) minus (15)]			$_____
(17) Total Spending against Budget [(15) minus (10)]			$_____

Strategy Summary Form - The Marketing Game!

Industry: _____   Firm: _____   Period: ____

Target Market(s): _____
_____
_____
_____

Product: _____
_____
_____
_____

Place: _____
_____
_____
_____

Promotion: _____
_____
_____
_____

Price: _____
_____
_____
_____

Competition: _____
_____
_____
_____
_____
_____

BUDGET PLANNING FORM for The Marketing Game!

******Financial Summary / Pro Forma ******

Industry: _____ Firm: _____ Period: _____ Brandname: _____

	Channel 1	Channel 2	Total
(1) Estimated Units Sold	_____	_____	_____
(2) Wholesale Price	$_____	$_____	
(3) Base Unit Cost	$_____	$_____	
(4) Gross Sales [(1) × (2)]	$_____	$_____	$_____
(5) Cost of Goods Sold [(1) × (3)]	$_____	$_____	$_____
(6) GROSS MARGIN [(4) minus (5)]			$_____

EXPENSES:

	Channel 1	Channel 2	Total
(7) Advertising			$_____
(8) Sales Force-Salary	$_____	$_____	$_____
(9) Sales Force-Firing Costs	$_____	$_____	$_____
(10) Sales Force-Commission	$_____	$_____	$_____
(11) Customer Service			$_____
(12) Sales Promotion	$_____	$_____	$_____
(13) R&D for Product Modification			$_____
(14) Marketing Research			$_____
(15) TOTAL EXPENSES [sum of (7) to (14)]			$_____
(16) Net Contribution to Profit or Loss [(6) minus (15)]			$_____
(17) Total Spending against Budget [(15) minus (10)]			$_____

Strategy Summary Form - The Marketing Game!

Industry: _____   Firm: _____   Period: ____

Target Market(s): _____
_____
_____
_____

Product: _____
_____
_____
_____

Place: _____
_____
_____
_____

Promotion: _____
_____
_____
_____

Price: _____
_____
_____
_____

Competition: _____
_____
_____
_____
_____
_____

BUDGET PLANNING FORM for The Marketing Game!

******Financial Summary / Pro Forma ******

Industry: _____ Firm: _____ Period: _____ Brandname: _____

	Channel 1	Channel 2	Total
(1) Estimated Units Sold	_____	_____	_____
(2) Wholesale Price	$_____	$_____	
(3) Base Unit Cost	$_____	$_____	
(4) Gross Sales [(1) × (2)]	$_____	$_____	$_____
(5) Cost of Goods Sold [(1) × (3)]	$_____	$_____	$_____
(6) GROSS MARGIN [(4) minus (5)]			$_____

EXPENSES:

	Channel 1	Channel 2	Total
(7) Advertising			$_____
(8) Sales Force-Salary	$_____	$_____	$_____
(9) Sales Force-Firing Costs	$_____	$_____	$_____
(10) Sales Force-Commission	$_____	$_____	$_____
(11) Customer Service			$_____
(12) Sales Promotion	$_____	$_____	$_____
(13) R&D for Product Modification			$_____
(14) Marketing Research			$_____
(15) TOTAL EXPENSES [sum of (7) to (14)]			$_____
(16) Net Contribution to Profit or Loss [(6) minus (15)]			$_____
(17) Total Spending against Budget [(15) minus (10)]			$_____

Strategy Summary Form - The Marketing Game!

Industry: _____   Firm: _____   Period: ____

Target Market(s): _____
_____
_____
_____

Product: _____
_____
_____
_____

Place: _____
_____
_____
_____

Promotion: _____
_____
_____
_____

Price: _____
_____
_____
_____

Competition: _____
_____
_____
_____
_____

Notes

Notes

Notes

Notes

Notes

Notes